To Mary

Luna Reed Rowe

You CAN Take It with You

A Southern Grandma Spills the Beans
about growing up
(and, consequently, growing OLD)
in the South

Essays by Lucia Peel Powe
Illustrations by V.C. Rogers

Outer Banks Publishing Group
Raleigh/Outer Banks

For information contact Outer Banks Publishing Group at

info@outerbankspublishing.com

Illustrations by V.C. Rogers
vcrogers@nc.rr.com

FIRST EDITION – February 2019

Library of Congress Control Number: 2019931112

ISBN 13 – 978-1-7320452-6-2
ISBN 10 – 1-7320452-6-7
eISBN – 978-0463268360

Dedicated

To my seven daughters and step-daughters:

Lucia Claire Peel, Williamston, NC
Sarah Margaret "Mimi" Peel Roughton, Hillsborough, NC
Sydney Eldridge Peel, Woodside, Knoxville, TN
Elizabeth Chase Peel-Solow, Durham, NC
Louise Powe Kelly, Woodland Hills, CA
Katherine Powe Dauchert, Durham, NC
Josephine Powe McGuire, Calabasas, CA

To the Reader

All the proceeds from sales of this book will go to KidzNotes, a nonprofit that helps at-risk children by teaching them to play classical music. KidzNotes is the Triangle branch of El Sistema ("The System"), which was founded in the 1970s in Caracas, Venezuela by Dr. José Antonio Abreu with eleven children in an abandoned garage. Since then, the program has helped open the eyes and ears of over two million of Venezuela's poorest children. It is now all over the world, though not yet in every country.

When we founded KidzNotes in Durham in 2008, it was the first El Sistema program in the Southern U.S. The following year we hired Katie Wyatt, a violist with the NC Symphony, as KidzNotes first director. Ms. Wyatt was one of ten musicians (out of more than 200 applicants from around the world) to be named an Abreu Fellow and trained in the El Sistema method at the New England Conservatory of Music in Boston. The classes she started in Durham and Raleigh now reach over 600 children a year, and she was recently named National

Director of El Sistema, USA. (The program is known as "KidzNotes" only in the Triangle area.)

In 2017, the national office of El Sistema moved from Boston to the School of Social Sciences at Duke University in Durham. Why there and not the Music Department? Because study after study has shown that classical-music training keeps at-risk, headed-for-prison young people IN school, OFF the streets, OFF drugs, OUT of gangs and OUT of prison!

The new director of KidzNotes in the Triangle is Nicholas Malinowski, an opera singer and music educator (and basketball player!), who was previously the Community Program Manager for the Seattle Opera.

I invite my readers and all other music-loving citizens to send their ideas, their prayers - and their donations - to:

KidzNotes, P.O. Box 200, Durham, NC 27707
(919) 321-4475

Visit their website at https://www.kidznotes.org/ to learn more.

Thank you so very much!
- Lucia Peel Powe

1

Andy Griffith and Me
(2016)

"What? Grandma, you knew Andy Griffith – star of The Andy Griffith Show?"

Well, darlin', not exactly. Here's how the "event" occurred:

The original big, amazing Bonner Bridge was being dedicated connecting Bodie Island and Pea Island in about — oh, who knows what year? Maybe around 1960, '55 ... over half-a-hundred years ago.

Your granddaddy was a North Carolina Senator (before Governor Terry Sanford appointed him a Superior Court Judge) and he was invited to sit in the grandstand with the state officials, governor on down, and I, can you believe, was invited to sit beside him and to sing "The Star-Spangled Banner" accompanied by the Manteo High School Band.

We were led to our nice seats in the front row and there, beside me, sat the TV and movie actor Andy Griffith. We introduced ourselves, all in good Southern order, and the program began.

As an aside (a mere aside), when the moment arrived for yours truly to rise and step before the microphone, the wind turned, very forcefully arriving from the land-side, blowing out to sea — big time! Ooo-kay. The band was between me on the grandstand and the ocean, with their music notes being blown towards the water and away from me! I could not hear a thing!

Did I look frightened? Shocked? Probably. So, I watched the band director's baton, tried to imagine the right Oh-oh-say-can-you-see... First note — and on key!

I glanced about to see if everyone was laughing. No one was. No one was looking at Grandma. I was shocked and relieved. So, following the baton's every cue, we arrived, all together, at the same note at the same time, my never having heard the band at all.

So, enough of that. Back to the real story.

First, Andy had grown up in Mt. Airy, N.C., graduated in acting, drama, theatre, you name it, from the University of North Carolina's Drama Department and had performed as Sir Walter Raleigh in The Lost Colony, in Manteo on the Outer Banks. He was capable of speaking the Queen's English. However, his career did not take off until he created, and made a hit recording of (are you ready?) "What It Wuz, Wuz Football!"

From there on, he went up, up, up, on TV and in movies; his longest-running character was as Sheriff Andy Taylor in his own program, a true family show, every week, while he spoke in a Southern small-town brogue: "'I'se right 'chere y'all."

All right. So, what happened on the grandstand that afternoon? Are you ready?

Miss North Carolina was brought aboard, introduced, and she gave a nice, brief welcome speech to all assembled. (The wind cooperated and did not blow her words away!)

Then, I overheard to my right (but pretended I did not hear it), I heard Andy lean over to the fella on his right (a Senator? a Judge?). "Hey" — as he pointed to Miss North Carolina's upper parts — "do you guess them thangs are real?"

I tried not to smile. Shocked! But trying so hard not to smile! ✦

2

Christmas Pageant
December 22, 1936
Trinity Avenue Presbyterian Church
Durham
(2013)

Two little five-year-old blonde angels, one of whom was me, wearing wings and halos, crawled on their hands and knees across the floor in front of the choir, the shepherds and the angels, Joseph and Mary to take a peek at the baby Jesus in the manger on the other side of the altar. They pulled themselves up, took a gander and were shocked! Plopping back down, they stared at one another, mouths open, shook their heads and started crawling back across. What had they seen in the small, wooden manger?

A pile of straw and a light bulb.

Sitting back down, one yawned. The other yawned. Then the first gave another great yawn. Members of the congregation started yawning, then the choir. People in the congregation started giggling, then the choir. Some members of the congregation started laughing out loud. That's when my mother had to stand up and leave, as she was mortally embarrassed.

Later, whenever Mama told this story, she always had to mention the "power of suggestion." If she were alive today, she would be 108 years old. If I, her "littlest angel," now 82, would try to correct her — as in, "Mama, the 'power of suggestion' could not possibly be that strong!" — she would merely smile at me. She knew better.

3

The Vet on the Bus
(2016)

Why is it that I cannot recall the names of important people, the titles of books, street names — but I cannot forget a five-minute event that I observed in 1944 when I was a mere 13 years old?

May I describe it? I was in the eighth grade at Needham Broughton High School in Raleigh, North Carolina. Every Monday and Thursday afternoon I had to catch a city bus after school to ride down Hillsborough Street to the State Capital, jump off and walk two blocks to my piano teacher's studio in her home in the Oakwood neighborhood.

One day, as usual, I sat down near the front. At the very next stop, the doors clanged open and there stood an African-American soldier in uniform, holding two crutches, one under each arm. One leg of his uniform was pinned up to the thigh. Obviously, there was no leg there.

He hesitated for a moment, studying how to let go of the crutches to grasp the metal handles on each side of the door and step up onto the bottom step of the bus — maybe one-and-a-half feet off the street. As he pondered how to accomplish this easy (for those of us with two legs and two available hands) task, I glanced at the bus driver to see if he might help.

He stared straight ahead down Hillsborough Street, never once even looking at the soldier. He wore a uniform, but it was not a military uniform.

I looked about at the others near the front, but they, too, were looking out the windows. As I was about to put my books aside and go help the soldier, he somehow, miraculously, managed to lift himself up that high step without falling back onto the sidewalk or losing his crutches.

After he put his nickel (remember, this was 1944!) into the slot — the same amount that I had paid — he sat down with relief beside me and searched for a place to put his crutches.

Before he caught his breath, the white bus driver jumped up, pointed to the back and shouted, "Boy, you get to the back of the bus!"

I froze.

The soldier jostled, scrambled himself up, gathered his crutches and before I could say, "Mr. Driver, let him have my seat and I will go to the back of the bus," the soldier had struggled halfway to the rear.

That moment stuck in my 13-year-old gizzard. It has never left. ✦

4
Grandmother's Mulberry Tree
(2008)

My mother's mother's house was built around 1870 or so with stones in the chimney bearing bullet holes from a Civil War skirmish nearby. The house still stands beside the original road between Atlanta and Marietta, Georgia.

In the side yard, during my childhood and beyond, was a very old mulberry tree with one heavy low limb that had broken partially loose and fallen toward the grass. To save the limb, my grandfather, before he died in 1933, found a heavy metal chain to tie to the main trunk and attached it to the outer end of the low limb. Whee!

We children could jump up on the old thick limb, hang onto the chain and swing, dance, wiggle, kick, hang loose, or fling our bodies over it and land on the ground. I hope this picture is clear.

I innocently played on that magical old tree, but never ate but one mulberry. Yuck. Besides, the ripe mulberries attracted yellow jackets!

When I was a junior in high school, a boyfriend dumped me just before Valentine's Day. I was devastated. I can still remember the painful tart-sweet odor of the strawberry-flavored lipstick that I was wearing at that time and can picture its dainty white tube.

One night, six months later, he came to see me at grandmother's house and asked me to go out and sit on the tree limb with him, where he asked to come back into my life, for me to "take him back." I still recall the yellow cotton sundress I was wearing.

Somehow, sitting on grandmom's big old tree limb, I was able to look him in the eye and say, "No, no. That time is over."

From that night on, I seemed to be able to control my life ... as far as men were concerned.

Unlike most of my friends, I did not marry until I was 26. They married during college or shortly thereafter. Probably I was considered an Old Maid at the time. When I did marry, I never suffered one regret.

Thank you, grandmother's mulberry tree. ✦

5

I Pity Pretty Girls Today
(2012)

I really pity any single girl today, pretty or not.

I already feel depressed merely approaching this subject — major cultural changes in society in the last half-century.

The saddest is the role of single women. While gaining their equal rights, they lost their magic.

If they date at all, they are expected, sooner or later, mostly sooner, to "put out."

How can a high school or college girl possibly discover who she is, what she thinks, stands for, what the purpose of her life may be, if she is encouraged to dress herself to attract the male of the species early on (13 years old?) while testosterone is banging around the space behind his eyes that was originally designed (let's not go there) to house a brain? Many models, such as in W magazine, are posed, exposed and dressed like pitiful streetwalkers in low, lace, see-through tops above tight, tight jeans, exposing navels, navels, navels. Is there anything sexy or interesting about a navel, that place where the umbilical cord was cut, pinched, chopped off? Whatever. Ugh. Who wants to look at one? Do boys really like to look at navels?

But I digress.

"In my day...." All right, but we had it so good. We had so much fun! Happy little virgins.

Never expected to do anything, to "put out," nothing. Not even a good-night kiss under the front porch light, if we didn't want to. We always double-dated, triple-dated, home by 10 (11 after ball games, 12 only after chaperoned dances, where we danced with everybody). I felt sorry for the girls who "went steady." That meant they probably had to kiss a lot and dance with only one boy all evening.

A certain group of us preferred to never go steady, but to date, one boy Friday night, another Saturday night, all in the same group — joke, joke, laugh, laugh, nothing vulgar. The guys never used four-letter functional words in our presence. I don't think they were in use then. Not even when I was in college. No one needed vulgarity nor cursing to make a point. Perhaps the guys respected us?

Why is it needed now? Maybe shrinking vocabularies require more cursing and vulgarity.

We cheerleaders wore knee-length full skirts that twirled when we turned, with long-sleeved "letter" sweaters over shirts with collars. One cheerleader was kicked off the squad for sitting in a boy's lap down on the front row of a basketball game. The principal explained to us that

we were supposed to "set an example" of appropriate be-
havior to younger students while representing our high
school in public at all times, in all places, even out of the
cheerleading uniform.

We felt safe, secure, special. Our parents, the school officials and the boys treated us like princesses. We loved it.
I liked saying, "Mother won't let me date the same boy
two nights in a row or stay out after a certain hour." Really,
what do kids talk about after 11 o'clock, anyway? The
guys felt obligated to "smooch," they called it then, and I
didn't care to kiss those boys on the mouth or, by today's
standards, in the mouth. Yeueew! Looking back, a few
boys might have seen matters a little differently, but I preferred to play dumb. Put everything off. It was possible, at
least then.

Now, boys today have so much thrown at them, visu-
ally, literally and figuratively, that they can truthfully say
to a girl, "No matter. If you won't, somebody else will. See
ya' later." For some years now, guys have been saying,
"Why pay for it when we can get it free ... from nice girls."
In fact, John Grisham treated that very subject in his com-
ing-of-age novel, The Painted House.

If we attended a party at a friend's house, the parents
were always present. So what? They were our friends, too.
We knew everyone's parents, from ball games, church,
band, concerts, scout troops.

Oh, and we'd never even heard of "co-ed" dorms! What
were the school people in the '70s thinking? Did they
think 18-year-olds checked their hormones at the front

door? I could almost believe that permissiveness was a dirty communist plot designed to ruin our younger college generation, take their minds off studying. I can assure you, it did. The schools said they were not responsible for the students. They were not intended to "parent" these kids. No dorm mothers. No sign-out books, no curfew, no rules. A girl could be dead in the woods a week and who would know? Her roommate might assume she was staying over in her boyfriend's room.

I'm not making this up. My eldest daughter, now an attorney, was in one of those dorms at UNC. (No telling who, or what might be in the bathrooms when I visited.) Boys' rooms on certain floors; girls on the others. But she had to leave the room we had paid for to study down the hall in her nightgown when her roomie, a nice Baptist girl, brought her boyfriend in and smiled at my daughter to exit. One night, she, my daughter, smiled back, continued to study on her bed, and the couple got huffy and went to his room; I assume they ran his roommate out. 1976. Consequences of the infamous '60s?

Six sociologists will offer you six different reasons for today's mixture of morals:

- Television and movies. Need I explain?
- The automobile. Parents have no idea where their daughters are, or with whom.
- Children growing up in large cities where they are nameless, rather than in small towns, known by all. "Alice, your girl Lucy was smoking behind the drug store after

school last week." It really does "take a village to raise a child."

• The music choices of the young; anything their parents do not appreciate or understand. Rock and Roll, now rap and hip-hop. Even the best parents don't listen to the words of the songs their precious daughters are playing in their private rooms. (Atlantic Monthly, Jan. 2006.)

• The church — any church — having less influence, competing with television, rap music, film, etc.

• An increasing percentage of young children with no father figure in the home, both African-American and white. Bad for both boys and girls. The daughters may be out early looking for a male to make them feel special, appreciated and loved, the role a good father might satisfy if he was present.

Are we to accept that "the hand that rocks the cradle" belongs to a lady with her boobs and belly button exposed?

Just overheard: Madonna does not want her daughters to see their own mother's movies!

Go figure. (2012) ✛

6

School Daze and Marriage
(2007)

Naah. There couldn't be any connection. Surely, the education we received, if any, during high school and the choice of whom we married had no possible connection. Certainly, the cute, happy friends we made during our sophomore, junior and senior years in secondary school had no bearing on which man we selected to wed, plan a family and make a future.

However, strange as it may seem, ironic perhaps, the puzzle pieces in my life did make a picture: My senior year at Marietta High School, I was one of the six cheerleaders. We were all friends but vaguely divided into two groups of three. Amy, Barbara, and Charlotte were so popular and cute. Called "ABC."

Amy: tiny, short, brunette, twinkling brown eyes, pretty lips, always had a steady boyfriend, one after the other.

Barbara: beautiful, shining, long black hair and bangs, dry wit, always had a steady.

Charlotte: short blond hair, a superb basketball player, pretty skin, totally unselfconscious, always had a regular boyfriend.

My group was "KLM": Katherine, Lucia, and Merrilyn. We had good times, too, but chose never to "go steady" or have a full-time boyfriend. We had to be home early after ballgames and dates. We'd date, but always, always double-date, going out with one boy Friday night for a ballgame, another Saturday night for a movie, and a third Sunday night for church youth group. No movies allowed Sunday nights. I might be with Jack on Friday night double-dating, and he'd be in the backseat Saturday night with my girlfriend double-dating again. And this was A-OK. So what? (Unless you had a secret crush on him.) All we ever did was laugh, eat, joke, eat, tease, eat — oh, yes, and no drinking. No sneaking beer, ever. Drugs? We didn't know what they were. Pot? Something to cook in.

Park? Mercy, no. For one thing, we might get "talked about." Particularly by the guy. So, we'd give him nothing to brag about — unless he was a liar.

"Smacky-mouth" was just not a necessity. We tried to hide our crushes if we had them. Do today's teens know what a "crush" is? They might call it "the hots." We were not so crude; young romantics, maybe.

No dating during the week, but lots, yes, hours, of talking on the phone. Actually, truth be known, my "special" called me when his homework was done, usually after 10 p.m. Oh, yes, he was smart, witty. Unfortunately, I couldn't concentrate to study until after he phoned — wondering if he would call. Okay, so I wasn't oblivious to someone special; I only tried to appear so. The kids have a phrase for that now, too: "playing it cool."

Later, in college, I was told my nickname had been "Snow Queen." And all the time I thought I was sweet and friendly to everybody. You can't win.

I'd like to think KLM was fun, too, but we agreed never to "go steady." One problem at the many dances in those years was that a girl would have to dance with her "steady" all night. Dear me. We chose to play the field, never settle. If we stayed home on a Saturday night occasionally, so be it. We read a book.

KLM all attended "church" colleges. Katherine attended Furman and married a Baptist minister — a fun Baptist if you will — and they had three children. Merrilyn and I graduated from an all-girls' Methodist school, Wesleyan, in Macon, Georgia, she in religious studies. Merrilyn later earned her Ph.D. at Boston College. I started in Christian education and later changed to a Bachelor of Fine Arts in Music and Drama.

Merrilyn married a business major, who was later Mayor of Marietta, and they reared five children. She taught religion at a prestigious Atlanta private school. I married an athletic Phi Beta Kappa lawyer, a North Carolina State Senator, later a Superior Court judge — all one man — with a winning sense of humor, and we had four children.

I don't recall where ABC went to college or even whether they did. But Amy married several times, once to her friend Charlotte's husband after she broke them up. Charlotte married two or three times, and at the last class reunion, I attended she was single again. So was Amy, but she refused to come to the banquet because Charlotte was there.

Barbara, poor dear, married once, came down with MS and was nursed by her sweet husband 'til she died. Among the threesome of ABC, there were only two or three children born.

Now here's the clincher: At Marietta High School's 40th reunion, six male classmates produced a skit in drag, "ABC-KLM." All were wearing cheerleader costumes, wigs, grapefruit inside borrowed bras, and makeup. Get this picture: Two of them had been our football co-captains. One of those, Sam Hensley, class president, went on to be captain of Georgia Tech's football team his senior year. Another, Robert West, was captain his senior year of the University of Georgia's football team. Each member of the group wore a large letter on the front of his cheerleader's sweater and together they spelled "A-B-C-K-L-M." They danced, sang, and cheered "Go, Devils!" because Marietta was the "Blue Devils."

The guys had written a song that asked "How did ABC have seven marriages and only two or three children? And how did KLM, the don't-touch-me, Goody-two-shoes girls, have only three marriages and twelve children?" Their winning premise seemed to be: "Since KLM never learned to kiss in high school, apparently they never figured out what made babies! Ha-ha, but I would add to that, "until they were settled with their husbands in a good home-life." And that may be the connection between School Daze and Marriage. ✦

7

Miss Jaw-jah, 1953
(2017)

Grandma Powe had no intention of mentioning the "Miss Georgia 1953" year in any form or fashion in this tome until her friend and former editor insisted, she do so.

Dr. Linda Hobson taught creative writing at LSU and other schools and was Executive Director of N.C. Writers Network when I served on the board, so she clearly knows more about what makes a book tick than I do.

So, how did Grandma Powe become Miss Georgia?

I was a graduating senior at Wesleyan College and Conservatory in Macon, Georgia, in the spring of 1953 and thrilled to have been cast as a performer in the very American play, Our Town, to tour through Europe that summer, playing in a number of universities where students were studying English (American style). However, the year before, a Wesleyan Conservatory piano student, Neva Jane Langley of Lakeland, Florida, had won Miss

Macon, Miss Georgia, and — R U ready? — Miss America 1952. Yeah!

So, the Miss America Pageant company was charging the Macon Junior Chamber of Commerce $1,000 to bring the former Miss Macon back to town for the Miss Macon 1953 pageant. That was a lot of money in 1953! The Jaycees came up the hill to the conservatory to beg for five girls to "puh-leeze" compete in their '53 pageant with five girls from Mercer University downtown. Sooo...

I said, "No."

My roommate, a piano major, wanted to do it and win a scholarship. (It was "all about the scholarships" then.) She said she would participate only if I would do it also, along with her.

I said, "No."

My mother said, "No. You're going to Europe this summer with your theatre department."

My roommate begged.

How do you tell your roomie to go jump in the ditch, "while I tour Europe"? So I agreed, knowing I would not win.

And we had to "do" a talent! I did not major or minor in piano or voice, but I sang a song — I forget what. (It was 64 years ago, remember?)

Guess what? I won the darn thing: "Miss Macon." I had to hang around that summer and touring Europe to prepare for the Miss Georgia Pageant. And lo and you-know-what, I won that.

Miracles do happen.

Friends told me that the reason I won those two events was that "you didn't even try!"

"Oh, I didn't?"

"No, you just ambled out on stage — not strutting, not marching, not 'Look at me! See my legs, my hair, my smile!' You just sorta suggested, 'Hi, y'all, how're you doing?'"

"Well, I'll be ...."

However, I did win two nice scholarships that helped pay off my college bills.

Here's another amusing part: There was no reason to go to Atlantic City for the '53 "Miss A" pageant, as there was no way the judges were going to give the title to a second Miss Georgia and a second Miss Macon from the little (450) student body of Wesleyan College and Conservatory up on the hill. But I had to go up there any way to represent our beautiful state. (And my mother chaperoned me.)

It was a delightful experience, meeting all those sweet girls from all over America, and a lovely girl from New Jersey won the "Miss A" title. She was the first entrant ever to win from New Jersey, where the pageant had been held for many years.

I am not sure the Miss America pageant exists anymore. I haven't seen it on television in many years. But then, I don't watch TV. Don't have time. I gave my set to our church's homeless center several years ago so the homeless could watch it.

I'd rather read. (And write?)

Hey, I'm not against television! I made my living on it, teaching Romper Room on a CBS TV station and writing commercial copy for advertisers. I've much to thank television for. So how could I knock television — y'all?

Just saying. ✦

8

Dinner Not Ready?
(2007)

How did my first husband, a Superior Court judge, ever survive being married to me? I still wonder and that dear man passed away many years ago.

He was so patient with me.

For instance, he might come home for dinner, often driving 80, 90 miles or so from Goldsboro or Kinston (when he wasn't assigned across the state in Charlotte or Asheville or Wilmington), and "dinner" might not be ready yet! I had no cook, but I/we did have four daughters. Sometimes one might help me, but they had Girl Scouts, band practice, choir practice, homework, piano practice, cheerleading practice, et cetera, rah, rah!

So, I mostly cooked alone — after leading a Scout troop, directing three church choirs, chairing a board or three, playing a bit of bridge (three different clubs), or what all.

Therefore, the exhausted Judge Junie Peel might pleasantly give me a hug, grab an apple from the fruit bowl, and go to the den to read the papers or catch up on his ever-present requirement to read all the new cases from the N.C. Superior Court, the N.C. Supreme Court and the U.S. Supreme Court (a judge cannot judge if he does not know what the law is, both present and past — just sayin'), 'til I summoned him and all the four girls to dinner.

(Law', me. I coulda never been a judge!)

I'm not even convinced I managed a house (home?) for six people, handling groceries, yard, shopping, church (three choirs!), cleaning — I had some help there — trips to Raleigh when husband served in the State Senate, being an active member of the Sir Walter Cabinet...

Well! I obviously was not the best bridge player in town. In fact, once when I said, "I can't remember who played that jack," a friend came back at me with, "Lucia, the fact is, you don't care jack who played that jack!" Can you believe a Southern lady would tell a friend such a rude thing?

✦

9

Junie Junior
(1995)

I was so against our naming our first baby, a girl, for me. I feared she might be required to live down my name or, more unlikely, live up to it. In any event, I did not want her to suffer more pressure than normal. My husband, however, Elbert Sidney Peel, Junior, insisted he would name her for me, Lucia Claire. So he did. Now we are known as "Big Lucia" and "Little Lucia." 'Course I'm Big Lucia. Fun, huh?

We did not wish to know the sex of our first baby, nor the second, until they arrived all red and squirming, "ongoing about" immediately for sustenance. Then only did we ever learn their sex. At the last visit with Dr. Rhodes before the full-term birth of the second baby, I forgot to mention to him that I had felt little or no kicking or movements the last week or so, and he failed to place the stethoscope to my middle to check movements and listen to the heartbeat.

The Day arrived, contractions began, and we phoned my mother in New Bern, 60 miles south, who already had her bag packed. My nextdoor neighbor, "Annie Bridge" Manning, stepped over; my elderly mother-in-law dropped by; and who knows who all else. They, we, decided not to call Daddy "Junie" yet, as he was sitting in the Senate session in the old capital in Raleigh and could drive home whenever called within two hours. Dr. Rhodes was down by the Pamlico River having a brief, well-deserved vacation, but his stand-in, Dr. Llewellyn, called us to drop on over to our community hospital, one block from our house. Yes, Williamston was Small-Town USA, and I'd give anything for it to remain just as it was. No chance, of course. (Well, it sorta has, actually.)

After a checkup, they settled me into a room with a relaxing pale pink (for its calming effect) walls. I overheard Dr. Llewellyn phone Junie in Raleigh to come on downhome ... and did I recognize a tone of urgency in his voice? Surely not.

Matters moved ahead quickly, I mean really fast. I was knocked out, "totally sedated," they called it. Now, mothers are often kept awake to help the action along. At any rate, when I woke up, I was back in the pink room. At my bedside was Daddy Junie, having driven the two-hour trip from Raleigh in one-and-a-half hours. Amazing he was not arrested, Senator or no. Also, my mother, his mother, doc, the nurse, Annie Bridge, and I can't recall who else. I asked, of course, "What is the baby? A boy or a girl?"

Silence.

Finally, somebody said, "A boy."

So I said, looking about, "Where is he?" Silence.

Then my husband leaned down close, hands on my shoulders, "Lucia, our baby was born dead."

So confused was I, still in a drugged haze, I asked them all, "How could he be born and dead? I mean, born means 'come alive'" ... I rambled on to myself.

No matter. It was so.

But he had been so active! Kicking and rolling about. I'd been sure that if it was a girl, she'd be a ballerina and if a boy, the place kicker for the Williamston High School Tigers. This, doc said, may have been the problem. The cord was wrapped around his neck ... so tight.

He was buried in the tiniest casket in the family plot, and today his father and grandparents are beside him, and someday I shall be.

A friend from out of town said, "Why don't you sue the doctor?" Everybody wants to sue the doc "for not checking the heartbeat on your last visit." We never ever thought of it. Largely because what if he had discovered the heart was not beating ... what could be done? Bring the dead baby on early? Not a good idea. May cause poison or infection, or some such to the mother. Nature takes her course and will deliver the fetus at the appropriate time, stillborn or alive, when all the amazing, magical hormones kick in together and announce, "Now is the time. Let's go, team."

God, the Creator, call that power what you like, I personally stand in total awe of the creative process ... of man and nature, the sea, clouds, heavens, and I'll go to my grave not believing it was created in six days by a blink of "His" eye or a pointed forefinger. Mystery, mastery, miraculous. How could my little brain possibly understand creation? Why should I even try? Not enough brain cells here.

If he had lived, I would surely have insisted on naming him for his father, another junior, and no doubt he would also have inherited his daddy's nickname, "Junie," or even, "Junie, Junior."

Also, had he lived, I might never have enjoyed Mimi, Sydney, and Elizabeth — Triple Treasures. ✦

10

Last Night's Dream
(2008)

I went to bed last night planning to write my essay about my "relationship to nature" this morning, April 1st. Yes, you-know-what's-day.

But during the night I had a dream or a message that somehow spoke to me, saying, "Loo-sha, you've already written that. Use it. About your river."

Clearly, I was being told to use the preface of my little novel, Roanoke Rock Muddle. It explains, somewhat, my love affair with the Roanoke River. What it does not explain is that it was my first husband's feelings about the river that started the whole thing. How as a little boy he'd come home from playing too near and even in the dangerous not-to-be-played-in river, with wet corduroy knickers and white shirt, to face a very upset mama, Fannye Myrt Manning Peel.

As an adult, an attorney, state senator and judge (oh, have I mentioned that already?), he would paddle or use a motorboat to take his father, Mr. Elbert Peel, an attorney also, fishing up and down the same "please-don't-fall-in" Roanoke River. "Junie" (Elbert Sidney Peel Jr.) didn't go for fishing so much as the quiet, the peace, the running river, the bird songs (225 species). He might hold a fishing rod in one hand but always had a book in the other. Both men had graduated Phi Beta Kappa from the University of North Carolina. (I mentioned that before, too, didn't I? But this is a collection of separate essays, right?)

Later, Junie tried to promote the river as the lifeblood of the valley to the business leaders in the area. Williamston would not be in that location at all except for the bend in the river. In the early years of our country, it served as a highway and railroad track, bringing by barge crops, cattle, equipment, mules, supplies, travelers, business, friends, entertainment. Not to mention supplying fish, such as herring and rock (striped) bass to be salted down in barrels for the winter (not the rock bass, but the herring). He felt the river should continue to serve as a blessing, bringing in fishermen from many counties, tourists who came for canoeing trips, birdwatchers, campers, hunters. Judge "Junie" Peel envisioned eco-tourism before the word was invented!

After he died, I became further concerned that, although the U.S. Corps of Engineers had declared it the swiftest, deepest river on the Eastern Seaboard and a "pristine" river, there is a sign near Plymouth stating: CHIL-DREN AND PREGNANT WOMEN: DO NOT EAT FISH FROM THE BOTTOM OF THIS RIVER. If our government insists this river is "pristine," we are in trouble.

Nevertheless, my daughter, Lucia Claire Peel, also an attorney, is presently chairman of the Roanoke River Partners. (Her father, Judge Peel, would be so pleased.) The river still suffers from hog-waste runoff and the lead, dioxin, and mercury dumped into her by industries upstream. And all the income from the sale of Roanoke Rock Muddle is now donated to Roanoke River Partners. ✦

11

Do We Dare?
(2008)

Do we dare, have we ever dared, to make fun of a person, child or adult, who is trying to speak clearly but cannot because of stuttering — that embarrassing trip-up of the tongue that prevents their message from emerging clearly, or immediately? Consider "F-f-f-f-ire!" or "W-w-w-watch o-out! A c-c-car is c-c-coming!" If I appear to be making light of this subject, I do apologize. But we can only imagine how frustrating this must be. Such as, "I-I-I love you, I-I-I think."

My first, no second, observation of stuttering came when my bright, inquisitive daughter, Mimi, at approximately age four-and-a-half, developed a stutter.

Her father and I took her to a speech therapist. I shudder to think of children and adult stutterers on this planet who have never heard of a speech therapist. How stuttering affects their lives, their grades, their self-confidence, their employment, their love life, their social life. "Speech impediment" is a very mild term for this problem.

The therapist told us something to the effect that she was quite bright and her mind and thoughts were moving faster than her lips and tongue could translate into words. We recalled how, as a two-year-old, Mimi sometimes yelled in frustration because, we later realized, she could not express just what she needed, wanted, or wished to communicate.

My first encounter with stuttering was while planning my wedding late in 1956 with the organist/choir director at First Methodist Church in New Bern. I said I wished to have an all-Bach wedding, music-wise (silly me). His compositions are so orderly, unlike me. Neat, but not gaudy, not sentimental.

However, our choir director had other plans for our nuptials. She had already invited a young Duke ministerial student to sing a solo, "Because," or something similar. He served a small church out in the country every weekend between his studies at the seminary. How could I say, "Well no, I don't think so."

"Furthermore," she added, as an afterthought, "he stutters."

"Ah," I stood thinking. Such a lovely all-Bach wedding, b-b-backing out the back door. Then she looked straight at me. "You know, of course, that" — now hear this — "stutterers don't stutter when they sing."

No, I did not know.

So, my wedding was to be used as therapy for her young friend. Know what? I didn't mind — wonderful me. No. Really, I thought it was great. He sang beautifully. We were all pleased.

This is not a science paper. But, having taught children from kindergarten through college, I am now convinced that music, particularly the study of classical music, celebrates and enhances the brain synapses, connecting the left brain and right brain. Music, particularly if dance is included, helps children improve their walking, moving, reading and writing skills. I have seen it work. Furthermore, their I.Q. and SAT scores are improved for the future.

Also, consider that mathematics and music are on the same side of the brain. This explains why so many scientists, doctors, mathematicians, and computer gurus are also musicians. Ask any group of weekend musicians what is their day job. You can almost bet that, in this area of North Carolina, you'll hear, "Computers at RTP," or, "Skin surgeon at Duke," or, "A math teacher at UNC," or "Engineer," "Research scientist," etc. Doctors advise expectant mothers to play classical, "brain" music (not "wiggle" music) for their babies, even in utero.

Do you know which comes first? The math-brain or the music-brain?

I, of course, do not.

But, either way, we should hasten to promote more, and early, classical music in the nursery, playroom, kindergarten, first grade and beyond.

Children get out your mother's pots, pans, and great big spoons. Let's march around in a circle, knees high, head back, singing, "Jack be nimble, Jack be quick, Jack jumps over...." (Also known as "Twinkle, Twinkle, Little Star.") Mozart's old tune — written when he was 6 years old! or some such. ✦

12

Dating at Sixty
(2008)

If one has been widowed at 52 and left with four daughters, one never seriously expects or intends to be remarried. Among other reasons, what intelligent man in his right mind would want to date, let alone marry, a woman with such serious ... uh, "baggage" (and I love each one to pieces) as four daughters.

Firstly, she will forever be distracted by their health, activities, who they're befriending, dating, marrying, grandchildren, their pets, jobs, houses, furniture. (Oh, how delicious lists are. How could we ever write an essay/memoir san lists?)

Should a woman of a certain age remarry, anyway? There is no way, in my world at least, that she can divorce her children and grandchildren — nor their dogs or cats. Nor her own mother, still with us.

With this in mind, a Zeta Psi fraternity brother of my deceased husband called from Raleigh to say that he wanted me to meet a friend of his. He'd have him, Dr. David McAllister, pick me up the following Sunday afternoon to come to a barbecue in their backyard. That sounded innocuous enough and safe. Okay.

The fella had gray hair, a slight gray beard, blue eyes and seemed right fun. The two men played in — get this — a Dixieland jazz band together. The host ran an "old Rolly" family real-estate company or some such and Dr. McAllister taught advanced computer science at North Carolina State University.

About the third time we went out, this time to a luncheon after church at a friend's house, he mentioned, "I didn't know Southern ladies could be so rude."

"Really? What happened? I asked.

"Two women came over to chat, I supposed, and one asked me, 'Dr. McAllister, what do you do?' When I said, 'Computer Science,' they nodded and walked away."

"Poor man, don't you understand? They had no idea what to say next."

"They might at least have asked ... uh ... yeah, I guess you're right."

Later, to my surprise, it turned out David was eleven years younger than I! I was 60. He was 49. "My stars, David, why didn't you tell me?" I exploded.

"Because you wouldn't have gone out with me," he defended.

"You are so right about that, man ... I mean, boy."

Nevertheless, at Thanksgiving, I was at the "shore," as northerners like to call it, with my mother, and he asked me if he and his sister, a surgical nurse, and her husband and daughter might come down and take mom and me out for Turkey-day dinner.

"Oh no... I mean, of course, you can come, but I'll be cooking for us. However, I'm cooking a large duck this year instead of a turkey. Come on down."

Dear reader, have you ever cooked a goose? A duck is very similar, I suppose. Because they fly thousands of miles way up high and float on cold lakes and ponds, they are protected by layers of fat. Many layers of fat. Your turkey pan will be up to its eyeballs with cups and cups of pure, undiluted goose grease.

My mother, to be helpful, suggested I cover the bird with a large brown paper sack, the purpose being to make the critter to cook evenly all the way through without burning on the outside. Of course, I followed grandma's advice.

However, she forgot to tell me to cut back on the cooking time.

So, my new jazzy "boyfriend" and his family and I piled in from a beach walk to check out the Thanksgiving duck.

Placing the pan on hot pads on the counter, we lifted the lid and there, lying in the grease was a pile of bones poking up out of a pool of pure fat. The flesh had all cooked off and slid off the bones, breast meat and all, down into the bottom.

"Wait, wait. Don't touch it! I've got to get my camera," David's sister said. She went racing to her room, followed by her laughing daughter, while my mother and I stood - aghast, embarrassed; well, astonished, to say the least.

Fortunately, the sweet-potato casserole, green beans with ham hock, grapefruit-gelatin-marshmallow salad, pecan pumpkin pies, etc. seemed acceptable. And the watermelon-rind pickles.

The husband of the photo-snapping nurse redeemed their little family when, on the beach later in our jeans, splashing along in the shallows, David informed them that I could (at age 60) turn cartwheels.

"Aw, come on, I don't believe it. Show us."

David insisted I do just that.

So what? I used to teach dancing to little girls. No big deal. So, like a good puppy, I rolled off three or four cartwheels on the wet, sandy beach. They were so shocked then, that I was embarrassed. The brother-in-law informed me that age 60 now had a totally different meaning for him. I was glad I could be of service.

Later, I introduced Dr. McAllister to a lady at our church.

"Why should I take her out?" he asked.

"Because she's bright, she teaches at North Carolina State - and she is your age!"

They have been married now fourteen years. ✦

13

Dating a Priest
(2017)

A quarter of a century ago, I was a widow living in Raleigh and attending Christ Episcopal Church. The wonderful, witty priest, Daniel Sapp, had been widowed also. (So, where are we going with this? Do not be alarmed.)

Dan had been a journalist, married, with children, when he decided to go to seminary to become an Episcopal priest. He was also a very good dancer! Mutual friends of ours proceeded to "fix us up." Well, we never truly "dated," but they would arrange for him to escort me, with them, to balls and galas — you know, events raising money for various charities. This was back in the day when men wore tuxedos to balls and galas.

So, about the third time he arrived to pick me up for such an event, I answered the door and he was standing on the porch, with his hands crossed behind his back, looking up and down the street.

"Dan, are you okay?" I asked.

"Lucia," he answered, "your neighbors are going to think you rent me!"

'Nuff said. ✦

14
A Southern Proposal
(2017)

My two husbands both had four-letter last names beginning with "P." The first, Judge Elbert Sidney Peel, Junior ("Junie" to all the world), passed away of cancer nine years before my second husband proposed to me. The second, Edward Knox Powe III ("E.K." to the world), had also lost his wife to cancer, several years before the event described here.

So, when E.K. proposed to me, he said — and I remember this as clearly as a church bell — "Lucia, if you'll marry me, you won't have to change the initials on your hand towels."

Is that a romantic Southern proposal, or what? ✦

15

Grandma's New Boyfriend
(2016)

A coupla' years ago my lawyer-daughter, Lucia Claire, and I had just returned to N.C. from New York having been invited to the New York-North Carolina Society annual Christmas Ball, which for a hundred years or more has been "thrown" (okay, held) to honor a leading N.C. citizen who has performed or created some outstanding position for our fair State. (Are you, dear reader, properly impressed?)

On our return, I overheard Lucia C. telling a friend, "Mama has a new boyfriend."

"Really? What's his name?"

"His name is Mr. Arthur Ritis."

I, Grandma, stepped in to correct her. "Sugar, you are mistaken. I am more involved with another boyfriend."

"Oh really, mama? What's his name?"

"His name is Mr. I.B. Profen."

Sadly, Grandma is still involved, somewhat, with both of them, Arthur and I.B. ✦

16

Infirmity
(2007)

Honest Injun. I never gave the word "infirmity" nor its meaning a second thought, not even a first thought, until I was almost 70. My mother was active 'til she died at 86, except for mild (translated: no oxygen tank) emphysema caused by smoking. She should have suffered lung cancer from smoking 60 years(!), but she did not. I was a member of the UNC Lineberger Cancer Research Board and asked the director, Dr. Joe Pagano, "Shouldn't they research my mother to discover why she did not succumb to cancer?" Valuable information, I would have thought, to study her superb immune system, but Joe laughed. Actually, she was only in the hospital once, to have her appendix removed. Like Mom, I was only "in hospital" (as the British say) five times. Four babies and one appendectomy. No, six times, once to deliver a full-term baby boy, born dead.

My father was a diabetic from age 25 until he died at 52, but he was not infirm. He gave himself insulin shots every so many hours, ate a healthy diet and drove himself to work every day when his health allowed him to work. Granted, he never played tennis or jogged, but he was never athletic, anyway. He preferred reading.

There was an infirmary at my boarding school (one year) and my college (four years), but I never entered them. Not once. I actually didn't know exactly where it was located on either campus.

My first husband's parents were active until their deaths, except for his mom's emphysema — just like my mother. All four of our parents smoked habitually, as did my second husband's parents. Clearly, this is why neither of my two husbands nor I chose to smoke. As a child, did you ever try to breathe in a car in the winter with two smokers and the windows rolled up? Don't even try it. Then, as I approached age 63, having been remarried about twelve months ... whammo! The fan was hit.

My dear, sweet, handsome, smart, kind husband developed "the shakes." His right hand and chin began to quiver when he sat still and relaxed. The neurologist said that it was a touch of Parkinson's disease, but he could live with it. And live with it he did. We did. Over 17 years experiencing its advance together. It is a neurological disease caused by lack of dopamine, a chemical neurotransmitter, the powerful, magical, God-given messenger that races from the brain through the nerves to the muscles, through all those synapses to instruct the muscle what to do — all in nanoseconds. (A neuroscientist is most welcome to correct Grandma if he or she sees fit.)

Without dopamine, the muscle is useless. The victim's brain sends the message to type that word, drive that car, chew that morsel, but the message never arrives. Some patients fail faster than others. Some shake with palsy much more than others. No case of Parkinson's is exactly like any other. Some survive longer than others. All eventually must give up driving, walking, dressing, feeding themselves, bathing themselves.

E.K. died at 89. I firmly believe that if he had not had this neurological catastrophe, he would have practiced law, which he loved, and continued jogging and playing tennis, until the end. Well, maybe senior tennis.

Studies show that when we are diagnosed with Parkinson's, we have already lost 80 percent of our dopamine level. We might all be walking about with this disability sneaking upon us but haven't hit the tipping point yet.

Another reason to hug somebody, hit that ball, take that walk, visit the Grand Canyon, call that old friend, make that donation — and write that will.

P.S. : E.K. played "walk-on" football at UNC for two-and-a-half seasons. Could it have caused his Parkinson's? Studies now prove that one-third of all football players are stricken earlier than normal with some form of brain damage: Dementia? Parkinson's? Cancer? Just sayin'. ✦

17

Paging Dr. Parkinson
(2008)

(Please forgive! This and the previous essay were written about one year apart and include some of the same information — and I'm too old to rewrite them, okay? Thank you.)

When Dr. Parkinson's disease appears at our door arriving uninvited into our lives, we suddenly insisted upon learning all that's written about what to expect, how to accept it, and how to live with it. We read books and magazines, went online, talked with other stricken families...

And, guess what? There's very little there. We must learn most of what we know by living with Parkinson's day-by-day. Very like a marriage. Each and every case is different.

When my husband's Duke neurologist said, "Ah, yes. E.K. has a touch of Parkinson's, but he can live with it," we wondered: "How well? How long?"

Later, when he had to give up driving, tennis, jogging, swimming, his speech slowing, slurring, his steps faltering, awkward, the doctor admitted, "Actually, we do not know what causes Parkinson's. Consequently, we don't know how to cure it. We can treat the symptoms, somewhat, for a while, slow its advance, maybe, in some cases. But a cure?"

A British physician, James Parkinson, first described the disease and its symptoms in 1817! He recognized the mask-like facial expression — or no expression at all — and rigidity of the muscles, combined with uncontrolled body spasms in some cases, jerking, palsied movements in others, shaking in most. He said he could recognize persons with this malady on the street even if they had not advanced to having uncontrollable movements. When asked how he could do this, he said they all appeared younger than other persons their age. This because the small muscles stop performing early on, those that create smiles and frowns or lifting the eyebrows, furrowing the forehead. This lack of small muscle usage allowed the facial skin to remain smooth and thus, youthful appearing.

As each case is different and develops at a different rate, some patients respond well to the accepted treatment, Levadopa, some less so or not at all.

So, what is Levodopa?

Dr. Parkinson had been long dead when researchers discovered the cause, but not what caused the "cause." The chemical dopamine, produced by a gland in the brain, carries the messages through the nerves to the muscles that say lift, write, throw, touch, etc. The nerves and muscles may be perfectly fine, but without receiving the message from the brain through the nerves to the muscles, nothing happens.

Dopamine is the messenger.

Levodopa is a fake form of this amazing hormone/chemical. Fake dopamine helps some patients, for a time, not totally, nor for long. Longer for some than others. The words "dopamine" and "levodopa" do not even appear in the 1967 edition of Webster's Third New Collegiate Dictionary, unabridged, five inches thick. I looked it up.

Recent studies inform us that when patients are diagnosed with Parkinson's they have already lost 80 percent of their dopamine level. Many of us could be walking about with Parkinson's, but it hasn't hit the tipping point yet where tremors and stiffness appear.

Trial surgeries have been successful for a few patients, where surgeons insert an artificial dopamine dispenser inside the brain. This manufactured levodopa (fake dopamine) is placed where the gland normally performs. However, most doctors refuse to attempt this procedure on patients over 60 years old, as they may not be able to withstand the surgery — and it might not work, anyway.

Surely, we have some clues as to what causes Parkinson's? Some say it is genetic. They also note that boxers and football players suffer Parkinson's more often than others because of possible blows to the head. Think Muhammad Ali.

As it happens, my husband did play football in prep school for three years and at the University of North Carolina (as a walk-on) for two years.

Others suggest breathing insecticides could cause it. A journalist wrote a book about his wife's Parkinson's and noted that she and her sister recall their mother shooting a flit gun all over, above, and around them in their bedroom at night to kill mosquitoes and roaches.

E.K., my husband, remembers his mother did the same at Wrightsville Beach every summer to kill mosquitoes back in the 1920s. I remember this also in the 1930s at home, at the beach, and in the mountains. But were the Parkinson's patients in colder, mosquito-less climates also exposed to insecticides such as DDT? Just a thought. Another theory is that it is caused by lead and other chemicals in the drinking water.

How does Parkinson's affect one's life? E.K. Powe and I married in 1993. Less than one year later, he developed a tremor in his right hand and in the jaw. His life began to change, obviously. Having been a runner since high school, his running slowed to a jog, then to a walk, then a limp. Having started tennis at age five and playing for over 70 years, he missed his favorite sport. Handwriting and speaking presented problems in his law practice. Symptoms of Alzheimer's appear in some patients and as with him. Unrelated to Parkinson's, he has lost total sight in the left eye and a partial loss in the right eye. (That is, they think it is unrelated.)

Amazingly, he has kept his patient and kind attitude and is in generally good spirits. * This is not true of every patient. Personally, I suspect I might have become bitter, resentful and mean as a snake. Fortunately, he has a very healthy appetite. Still, as always, he was a gentleman and though smiling is difficult, he enjoys a witty remark and a good Carolina ball game.

Another sad point: Having been an oenophile since introduced to French wines in Alsace Lorraine during World War II, he is now not allowed alcoholic beverages. This is especially sad because studies show that red wine, in particular, has healthy properties for the heart and arteries because it contains resveratrol from the skins of red grapes. Occasionally he will accept a non-alcoholic beer. But we have not found an interesting non-alcoholic wine. Does the reader have a suggestion?

So, what does a restricted oenophile drink? Consider V8 juice, grapefruit juice, grape juice with Certo (fruit pectin for the joints), or carbonated water. He does not complain. He accepts this also.

Transportation? Of course, he cannot drive a car. This means that Mrs. Powe has been the designated driver for many years. Consequently, she too has accepted a lifestyle change. Well, one of many changes and she is not here to complain. Considering the driver, Mrs. Powe is approaching 77 years of age, Mr. Powe's family requests — demands — she does not drive her husband out of town. To the doctor's office, out to dinner, the occasional movie, yes. Which explains why the Powe's trips to their condo at the beach and visits to the mountains have stopped except when someone else is available to drive. All our "someone else's" have very busy active lives of their own, as indeed they should.

Our seven children (his three daughters, my four daughters) are very loving and accepting of the situation and helpful whenever they can be. The only ending I can offer for a non-medical essay about Parkinson's disease is a large question mark. So, here it is:

(Footnote: * E.K. was still alive when this essay was written. He died in 2011.)

18

Gray Matters, or Afterthoughts
(2010)

Question: What do the "elderly" think about? Who knows? Or can remember it? Or cares? An hour later they don't remember it themselves. Let's try the alphabet (if I can remember it):

A — Aspirin, arthritis, acetaminophen (did I spell that right?)
    B — Belching, bridge, bones
    C — Cholesterol, children, cruises, caskets
    D — Doctors!
    E — Ephedrine
    F — Fainting, feet, facelifts, funerals
    G — Grandchildren, geriatrics, gossip ... gas
    H — Hair (if any left)

I — Indigestion, insurance, ibuprofen, investments (if any left)

J — Jokes

K — Knees, kinesthetics (I forgot what that means)

L — Lap-bands

M — Medications, Medicare, memory, meditation, massages

N — Names? Nurses

O — Operations

P — Psychotherapy, prayer (that's obvious)

Q — Quitting, quilting

R — Rest, rest homes, retirement

S — Sex (whazzat?)

T — TV, tremors

U — "Undertakers" (who coined that word?)

V — Vaporizers

W — Wine, whine, wine

X — X-rays (bones, hips, knees, brain, etc.)

Y — You name it!

Z — Zantac.

Whee! What did I leave out? Oh! Food, meals, desserts ... oh, well. ✦

19

Let Us Now Praise Famous Gestures
(20??)

Gestures: a language all their own. A most powerful language, a visual, voiceless, silent language. The simplest gesture can denote love or hate, admiration or disdain, pleasure or boredom, pride or humility, physical attraction or abhorrence, anger or patience, lust or purity, power or weakness, self-confidence or embarrassment — and we won't even mention the flutter of eyelashes or the bold, burning, unblinking stare.

We're not taking the SAT here, so let's move on and make a visit to six, only six, classic gestures:

The first, number one, should be the right forefinger pointed to the sky. What else but "Numero Uno," "Number One," usually used in an athletic context accompanied by a large, toothy grin declaring, "We're number one!" Except in medieval and early Renaissance painting. An artist of the period, perhaps Flemish, Italian, or German, would depict a famous cardinal, bishop, or saint looking out at the viewer with the right forefinger pointed skyward. The meaning clearly was not "We're number one!" but "He is number one," and you'll find no smiles there. The painter and his patron were serious about the meaning of this gesture, giving the glory to God alone.

Second, let's turn to the gesture of the third finger and forefinger raised in a "V" for Victory and always coupled with a smile. In fact, a "V" is rather like a smile, right? It is turned up at the corners. But "V" does not indicate victory all over the world. No. In most of the world, languages are used that are not based on the Roman alphabet. In most languages that did not come down to the present through the Latin and the Germanic. For instance, in Chinese and Japanese, the letter "V" does not exist. What would the "V"-for-Victory gesture mean to them? My personal first recollection of the "V" sign was during World War II, seeing in black and white newsreels Americans riding on rumbling tanks down village streets in France and Germany flashing big smiles and the "V" gesture, done always with the right hand. Right? I now wonder, for only a moment, what the German soldiers flashed for their cameras as they were first moving out of Germany and into Poland, Austria, France. They do have a "V" in their alphabet, as used in "verboten."

The third gesture in my memory came to us with the Nazi Germans, their right hands and arms thrust out in front like toy soldiers to declare "Hail Hitler." Or as they spelled it, "Heil Hitler," meaning "We praise, honor, admire, trust, and follow you ... anywhere you lead us." And that they did. Also, I do not recall ever seeing a smile attend "Heil Hitler" in the fuzzy filmstrips we were shown in school when I was 11 to 14. I don't think the Nazi propaganda aces made this up, the gesture of the raised arm and hand as if saluting the sun. I'm inclined to feel it began with the Egyptians or earlier and was surely used by the Greeks and Romans in saluting their emperors and kings.

Not much new under this old sun. But the Nazis used it to a fair thee well. When we naive Americans first saw them perform this "Heil Hitler" salute, we smiled at the awkwardness of it: "Silly folks," we said. But no smiles later when we saw how power, racism, and blind devotion could lead an intelligent, literate society to perform such atrocities as were never conjured up in the most horrible of horror stories, movies, or even horror comic books: six million human beings killed. (If Jesus had lived in Germany then, they would have murdered him also.)

A fourth famous gesture in the western world is the use of the sign of the cross over a person's head. Performed by a Christian priest it can mean, "Your sins are forgiven. Go and sin no more." Over a dying person, used at the Last Rites, it means, "You are entering the Kingdom of Heaven. God bless your soul." When a harried mother crosses herself, it often means, "God help us all (and be quick about it!)." When someone uses a naughty, dirty word or curses and uses the Lord's name in vain and another person nearby crosses himself, it means, perhaps, "Forgive them, God," or, "Deliver me from such vulgarities. Help me rise above it (or above them). And remember, I didn't say that naughty word. I am Your good child."

It is difficult to think that most of our world's people are not familiar with Christ or God as we interpret and understand Him. To millions upon millions of Hindus in India; Muslims in the Near East, Central Asia and India;

Buddhists and Confucianists in China; Buddhists in Japan; and Africans with their many faiths, our gesture of crossing ourselves as a holy blessing is lost upon all of them.

However, two gestures are always, everywhere understood by persons of every race and faith: the fearful frown and the happy smile. They are depicted on ancient masks from early societies on every continent. Babies of every race and color learn to smile from seeing a smile. They respond in kind to their parents' smiles or frowns.

One study indicates that first-born children generally smile less all their lives because when they first looked into the face of their mother, she, being new at bathing, changing, dressing, feeding, was often observed not smiling as she was trying to learn how to accomplish these tasks. The child remembers his first viewing of her face. However, her subsequent babies looked up from their cribs and saw a smiling, confident, assured mother who knew exactly what she was doing. So in a sense, the baby's first viewing of mother's face is imprinted on his brain, his nervous system, you name it, and it lasts all his life. These are the two simple gestures, numbers five and six, then, that are recognized on every continent.

Oops-a-daisy! This is a doozy of a gesture I've nearly forgotten. One more gesture is understood on every continent. For a while, I thought it had vanished from our ken. I'd not even seen it on the playground or in movies, but it has made a dramatic comeback in the last three years. It has no name, but it consists of the right forefinger placed under the left ear and dragged under the throat up to the right ear. The seventh gesture, not a lucky sign at all. ✦

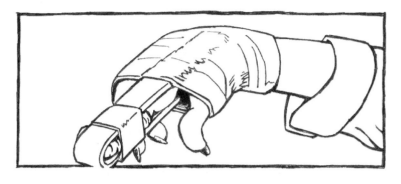

20

My First and Last "Bird"
(20??)

I can just see him now, my first husband, Judge "Junie" Peel, up there in heaven. Not resting in peace, dear no, but laughing his buttons off with his younger brother, Billy Bob — William Robert Peel — and his mama and daddy, Elbert and Fannie Myrt. They all loved to hear or tell a good story.

In Williamston, North Carolina, Mr. Elbert, right in the middle of teaching a Sunday School lesson, might recall some joke on the subject in the lesson — Trust or Forgiveness, say — and he just had to tell it. Right that minute. Then laugh and laugh. Judge Junie, too; they both taught Sunday School. Lord love 'em.

All three of these men were lawyers, which may or may not explain their drive to tell stories, and Junie was a Superior Court judge for 22 years. Even that dreary work did not destroy his wonderful sense of the ridiculous. Probably fed it with the preposterous truths and lies he heard from the bench — both offered up as equal-opportunity stories.

In 1984, on the last day he lived, knowing each day could be his last, Junie looked from his bed out the window and with a perfectly straight face, said calmly, "If they had told me I had lung cancer, I'd have been mad." He had never smoked tobacco in his life.

He died that night of pancreatic cancer. *

But his sense of humor lives on in his four daughters — and in my undimmed memories of him. Judge Junie told me once, "Lucia, you don't think anything is worth doing if you can't overdo it."

Well, I tried not to let that hurt my feelings. But wouldn't he be proud, so proud, of how I finally developed the ability to "shoot the bird?"

Rushing out to church Sunday last, to be a greeter, I pulled the door behind me and managed — somebody please tell me how — to leave the end of my right forefinger in the door-jamb.

With blood spurting all over the foyer of my house, I had to stretch out on the floor like some dunce because the other choice was to fall down on the floor in a bloody faint. E.K., my present husband, brought me a dish towel to staunch the bleeding and I begged him, "Please call St. Phillip's that I won't be shaking hands today. Sorry."

The handsome young Duke doctor in the Emergency Room wanted to remove the entire nail and, get this, stitch up the split nail-head beneath it.

"So, it will grow out pretty," he said.

I forthwith reminded him, "That form of torture is used by the Taliban on women who expose an inch of an ankle." I hid my hand behind my back and said, "We will just let Nature take its course."

Her course.

He seemed displeased with me, so I asked, "What would you tell your mother?"

"I'd tell her the same thing." Then he smiled. "But she wouldn't let me do it, either." So there.

However, to have the last word, he proceeded to install this giant-sized, overdone, impossible-to-ignore, shiny metal splint on the finger and strode out.

I did not "flip the bird" to his back.

The next night, I had my class at UNC and, wishing to be friendly and all, what could I do? I held up my splintered finger and explained how the accident occurred.

Furthermore, I had even worn my new silver bracelet to enhance the big, shiny splint. In overdoing this terrible effect, I was mortified; they, to a person, laughed. Then, in an instant, I saw why: the "bird!" In showing my splint, as it turns out, I ended up "shooting the bird" at 23 UNC students and one faculty person, our instructor.

In my seventy-and-a-half years on this earth, I had never, not once (like Junie never smoked), "flipped the bird." Perhaps it wasn't in my repertoire or I didn't know what it meant. Truth be told, it just never occurred to me to do so.

Why should I "shoot a bird" at anyone, even at a crazy speeder racing by me and my grandbabies, trying to run us off the road and into a culvert?

To top this terrible gaffe, on Tuesday evening, my baby daughter, a former UNC student, asked me, a little embarrassed —a lot embarrassed — "Mother, show me how you did it." So, I did.

And she fell out laughing, just like the class had. Like Junie and the Peels might also be doing in heaven.

"Mama, you didn't even do it right. You shot it upside down! And, it's the wrong finger!" •

(Footnote: * - Which, 30 years later, we still cannot beat. We put a man on the Moon nearly half a century ago and still cannot cure cancer. - 2017) ✚

21

Loafers
(2017)

Why do I so love loafers?

And I'm not talking about lazy men! I'm talking about the standard brown or black (usually) leather loafers birthed right here in the U.S of A.

And because I am addicted to lists, here are a few of the reasons why I love them:

1. They are worn (revered?) by both males and females.
2. And by people of every race under the sun.
3. CEOs and garbage collectors alike wear loafers.
4. As well as children and teenagers ... and even the elderly, like me!

What makes loafers so quintessentially "American"? Because their ancestor, obviously, was the American Indians' moccasin. The Indians knew how to wrap the deerskin under and around the foot and attach it to the top piece with thin strips of the leather, thus tying the top to the bottom.

Think about it, y'all. The early Indian moccasin is the great-great-granddaddy of our beloved loafer.

I've just counted in my closet:

• Six pairs of moccasins: brown, black, light blue, red, gray suede, and brown and white.

• And nine pairs (this is embarrassing!) of loafers ... mostly black – some suede, some regular leather –but also in brown, white, chocolate, and tan.

• And that's not even counting all the pairs my daughter tells me I wore for a while and then passed along to her and her sisters.

Several of these pairs of loafers I'm looking at now may be over 50 years old – well over, in fact! (I'm 87 at the time this book was published). And re-soled several times. (Right now, I'm wearing a black suede pair I bought in Denmark 25 years ago.)

So, does Grandma ever wear high heels? Goodness no! She used to, but now she might fall off of them – and break a hip.

My "dressy" shoes are a simple pair of black patent loafers — safe rubber soles, not slippery leather ones. Occasionally I'll snap a little silver buckle on top if I'm going somewhere really special.

We assume that ultra-high heels were designed to attract the eye to a lady's pretty feet, toes, ankles – to her long, lovely legs.

Presumably to aid in the continuation of the human race?

Ah well, as I approach 90 years of age, there is no reason – none I can think of, anyway – to try to attract anyone's eyes to Grandma's "foots."

Therefore, Long Live Loafers! ✦

22

Grandma's Veggie-Tini
(2017)

Often, I receive a quaint smile from folks when they ask, "Grandma, what is that cocktail?" — in a metal martini glass (unbreakable) with a slice of cucumber stuck on the side.

So, while pushing 90 — okay, only 87 — years old, here's the silly, boring story.

Ever since my brilliant lawyer-daughter turned off my stove so "you won't burn up the place," I am forced — forced, you hear — to eat out!

As I am also not allowed to drive at night, I am forced to walk one-half block to the nearest restaurant which just happens to be Paradise — uh, no, Parizade — just off Main Street in Durham, North Carolina. Ah, such punishment!

So, with or without friends or family, I deposit myself almost nightly there unless I am invited elsewhere (homes, or the many other amazing dining dens in Durham). And, hear this as my foot enters the door, the barista starts smashing her/his basil for Grandma Powe's healthy (you understand) Veggie-tini: a basil-cucumber martini. (What kind of alcohol may be in there? I have no idea.)

Oh, I have only "a half," you understand. Later, maybe, I might accept the other half.

It is a healthy potion full of "green" vitamins that we are convinced may keep us healthy, friendly and coming back — to Parizade.

P.S.: My son-in-law, Woody Woodside, in Knoxville, Tennessee, advises, "Keep up ordering the two halves. They might actually equal one and a half, for which you are only charged for one." We are a stingy family, ain't we? (Did he learn that as a young fraternity brother at N.C. State?) ✦

23

The 7th Commandment of Dining Out
(1996)

While flying above the Atlantic Ocean some years ago from Barcelona, Spain, to New York with my husband and a group of tired Durham friends, I happened to pick up Reader's Digest and it fell open to an article by a New York gourmet chef-type fella' named Bourdain. Anthony Bourdain.

I can't swear to the exact title of the piece, but he listed ten rules to memorize before leaving home to eat somewhere else. Ho hum. I assumed I already knew (being an Aries and a first-born only child) anything he wanted to tell me.

Well.

Commandment No. 7 almost knocked me out of my window seat: "Thou shalt not eat shellfish on a Monday."

Then he gently explained that world over, fresh (that is, not frozen) seafood, shellfish included, is always delivered to restaurants on Tuesdays and Fridays. So there.

The wonders from the sea on your plate have been lolling around somewhere back there, we assume, on ice, since last Friday .... and we don't know how long they were waiting in a boat somewhere before they were brought to shore and shipped, somehow, to your restaurant, now do we?

Bong! The Monday night a week before, in a hotel at a seaside village in Portugal, I spent the ghastliest night of my life. Pain, rumblings, roarings in the mid-section, up all night. I will not punish the reader with a serious medical description. Oh, my first husband called it the "green-apple quick steps." Of course, he was a Judge, not a doctor. The only thing good about that night was that my second husband slept soundly like a good puppy all night long.

Next day on the bus to Lisbon to fly over to Morocco we found that one of our tour leaders had been and was still very ill. So, we compared notes. We were the only two of the group who had ordered at the seaside restaurant a Portuguese Mussel Stew.

He was right! That darn Noo Yawk chef was so right!

But, wouldn't you know, always fascinated by the idea of eating something from the sea that we don't find on every menu, a few months later I totally forgot the rock-star chef's advice and did it again back here in North Carolina – two-and-a-half hours from the ocean – and suffered a similar but not quite so severe night. No sleep, as in Portugal. Dear darn.

Why can't some people learn anything? A friend of mine said that she would rather have a baby than have food poisoning. ✦

24

"Red Wine"
(2017)

Several years ago, my lawyer-daughter and I were having lunch at a small cafe on the outskirts of a little Southern town when the waitress asked if I'd like a beer or wine. When I answered, "Thank you, I'll have Pinot Noir," she apologized and said, "I'm sorry, Ma'am, we only serve red or white."

"Fine, I'll have the red."

When she had vanished to the kitchen, my daughter burst out laughing! "Mama! I am so proud of you!"

"Why?" I mumbled.

"You did not laugh – or even smile!"

Well. Aren't we pleased as punch when a grown daughter can say she is proud of us? ✦

25

Mechanical Moron, the Cliché (2005)

No first-born person, particularly a first-born only child, especially if they are born in April as an Aries, ever expects to grow up to be a cliché, one of many, a mere unoriginal repeat. Mom and Dad never prepared this special and only little girl, probably spoiled, to be one of the crowd. By spoiled, I don't mean in material items but by having more attention, more listening-to, than most children receive when they are one of several.

So here, when I can't make a cell phone, computer, TV, microwave, you name it, do its thing, and mumble, "I'm just a mechanical moron," my children, husband, step-children, friends, and repairmen are not impressed or even amused. "No. You don't even try, Mom," my daughters say. "You expect somebody to do it for you. You're just impatient. You want it to work right — and to work right now."

They are absolutely wrong. My family cannot, but I can clearly hear in these "techno" products the little demon spirits that inhabit them laugh as they see me coming. They all enjoy a great howl, slapping their buttons and knobs together. "Are we gonna show her? Go, team! Let's destroy her!" As you can see, "logical" in the word "technological" is a joke: These products are nothing of the kind.

So show me, they do! "Lucia can't even find the Power button to turn us on. Of course, we've hidden it — hee-hee-hee." That was the official techno-demon laugh. Here's just one example: If the remote is not handy — and it never is — I have to lean down "arse over elbows" to search for the Power button somewhere on the floor, and that button is black-on-black making it a devil of a thing to see. Chalk up one more for the little demon spirits.

I'd always assumed I had an okay I.Q. because some teacher — no, the principal — told me I did. Meaning I should be making all A's and thus helping to raise the school's academic curve. Instead, this made me feel guilty (easy to do to first-born children). Apparently, I.Q. has nothing to do with being able to make machines work. How do I know? Where did I get that idea? Because I was smart enough (or dumb enough) to teach English, creative writing, speech, drama, music, and filmmaking.

The sheriff's son was in my writing class one year and he could barely read, much less write a complete sentence. How he arrived at his junior year is still a mystery. Once there, he would often skip my class! One day when he was again missing, I left my students with somebody and hiked out down the hall in search of the high sheriff's son. Having received a tip, I discovered him out in a large, cold, dark garage being used for an auto mechanics class. The students all had their "sit-downs" up in the air, like Uncle Dub in "Kudzu," tinkering patiently with buttons, knobs, motors, electric wires, gasoline gauges, valves, and other parts I'm not sure the sheriff's boy could either pronounce or spell — but he could make them perform!

When I hailed him cheerily from behind, he rose up out of the gizzard of that old donated Ford, turned to me, all greased up and grinning, and didn't say a word, just kept smiling like he had found the Lord and wanted to share Him with me. Psychiatrists have names for this phenomenon, such as the left-brain, right-brain theory. I'm inclined to believe that we are born — the sheriff's boy and I — with certain talents already etched out right there in our DNA. You don't agree? Take one look or listen to those enviable people who can play piano "by ear." How the heck else can they do that other than by an inborn talent.

They tell me that math, music, science, and the "techno" arts are on one side of the brain and that the "creative genes" for art, literature, and poetry are on the other. A few people have developed both sides. How else can we explain the mathematically minded musician composing beautiful, artistic, poetic works of music? Well, we don't explain it. We just enjoy it.

You should see the startled faces of those who ask for my email address ... and discover I don't have one (Well, I finally acquired one – luciapeelpowe@gmail.com). I don't "do" computer. I'd rather call a person on the phone and enjoy the timbre of their voice, and not have to wonder if they have checked their 75 messages today, mine included, along with those from ex-Senator Bob Dole's Viagra pharma company.

I hereby admit that my understanding of the workings of the internet, TV, radio, X-ray, and CAT-scan is zero, but I accept them as I do Santa Claus, the Easter Bunny and the tooth fairy. However, I do feel a vast and warm debt of gratitude to A. Graham Bell. I do adore the telephone (smiley face). At home, in the car, on the beach, my cell phone is an umbilical cord to the outside world. Do you hear my four daughters and two husbands (both of them in heaven) laughing?

I do wonder how anyone survived before the telephone was invented! How the pioneers ever made it to the West Coast without phoning ahead for reservations, checking 'round the mountain to learn where the Indians were hiding, calling a doctor to come deliver their babies by some dry gully during a rest stop, ordering in their creamed cornmeal, buttermilk, sugar, and coffee? And how did we ever win the Revolutionary War against the mighty British without some primitive techno-instruments such as radios, walkie-talkies, electricity? Until the telegraph was invented in time to help Abraham Lincoln administer the Civil War, no general or president ever knew where anybody else was, friend or foe — behind a rock, deep in a forest, or over in the next state.

And now comes that still, small voice asking how many civilizations before us (Atlantis?) rose up, learned nature's techno-secrets, broke the codes and used them to their advantage, as with atomic power today, only to finally destroy themselves trying to play God. Funny — I can still hear those little devil-spirits laugh as they hunch together on the circular tray inside my microwave! ✦

26

Retirement Ain't What It Used to Be
(2019)

Growing up in the '30s and '40s, I pictured what retirement appeared to be. Something like: Stop teaching, nursing, carrying the mail, doctoring, selling insurance, and move to Tarpon Springs, Florida, because the state of Florida takes less of one's leftovers in taxes away from one's children. There, the husband plans to play a little golf, fish a bit and swim. (He never swims.) The wife is sure she will play bridge and shop a lot (which she does) and thinks she will swim, sew and catch up on her letter writing and memoirs (which she does not).

Two-thousand-nineteen. Retirement is here. What I find is ten different horses running off in ten directions. Which one to ride? Shall we list? ("God, why do I love to make lists?" God: "Because it fills up space and because you have ADD.")

- Deal with insurance

- Decide to stay in residence

- Deal with taxes

- Decide to move to a retirement community

- Deal with a pension, retirement funds, money, if any

- Move to a retirement community (no small undertaking)

- Deal with children and grandchildren

- Deal with doctors, dentists, neurologists, urologists, gynecologists, eye docs, foot docs, carcinoma docs, etc.

- Travel to countries with modern medicine or visit exotic areas with no medicine at all (wondering if one's friends are properly impressed with one's experiences), or ...

- Stay home and attend friends' funerals!

Three days ago, however, a funny thing happened to me that opened another whole modern view of what people can do today that they could not do in retirement in the '30s.

I innocently picked up the phone to call my daughter-in-law in Malibu, California, and dialed 888 instead of 818 as a prefix, and all a' sudden I was listening to the most, uh, insinuating, husky, breathy-sounding, female voice telling me stuff I had never heard of and what I could do ... I sit here now, turning red just thinking about it. Lord, a' me. What kind of woman was that? Was she really some mother's little girl? Somebody's sister or girlfriend? Some daddy's darling daughter? Was this the only way she could pay for her groceries? I thought I'd wait 'til a real person came on the line, as they often do, and insist they take our name off their list and never, ever, ever phone my home again.

Blushing all over, I realized ... she didn't call me. I had called her.

By then her oozing voice was breathing that I should take out my credit card and stick ... around for some real thrills. I am not making this up. I could not listen anymore. For a moment, I thought about using the card to tell them I would be forced to call the authorities and report this use of the U.S. of A.'s government-controlled phone lines. I could not believe this was legal. Was my tax money being used in any possible way to build telephone poles and wires to carry something as disgusting as this? Is this how we translate "free speech?"

Oh, we don't even use poles and wires anymore. Right? Well, whatever. Please don't tell me businesses are making profits using my beloved telephone service in such a manner.

At the risk of preaching or polarizing, might I just ask, "What if one of our four grandsons had accidentally misdialed as I had? What if young people at parties should all get on phones together and get an 'education' in this?" Anyway, I did not stay on the line or use my card to tell the company or whatever they were, a thing or two.

Good thing.

I left a message on another daughter-in-law's phone telling her what I had done. She called back later, howling with laughter. Thought it was so hilarious. Told me it was just as well I had not used my card because if our phone calls had to be checked for any reason (Who knows why? If someone stole our credit card?), they might have discovered that purple number on her father's charge list. Katherine seemed to think that would be terribly amusing. She also laughed because she said that I don't usually have such difficulty whipping out my credit card to follow an urge to buy. Unfortunately, that might be true.

And, frankly, it was Katherine Powe Dauchert's idea, when I mentioned I needed to sit down and come up with an essay about retirement, that I use this event to describe what could take place in modern "retirement" venues.

When grandma steps off to shop at Target, play bridge, take her Spanish lesson, and thinks grandpa is staying home to watch the baseball game or trim his roses (or his nose hairs), how does she know he is not dialing 888? ✦

27

Rather Read Than Eat
(Hmm? Okay, Rather Read than Sleep)
(2006)

Call it escape reading if you wish, except I never — well, hardly ever — read romances, murder mysteries, sci-fi or slasher novels. Occasionally I'll be reading a book like Nicholas Sparks' Message In A Bottle because the author is from New Bern, North Carolina, and all of a sudden I realize, "Oh, geez, this is another romance. Duh." I'm not disparaging romances. They make a good living for their authors and they help the G.N.P. But my little life is too short to expend that many hours indulging, knowing that the Girl Gets the Guy, in the end, most times — though not in Gone with the Wind, nor in Message in A Bottle. (Nor in my little novel, Roanoke Rock Muddle.)

For a Lifetime Learning class at Duke University, I was asked to write about the following:

(1) "What Reading Has Meant In Your Life." My title answered that. My husband might say, "Reading IS her life."

(2) "Writers That Have Affected, Touched You." Lloyd C. Douglas; I read his Magnificent Obsession when I was 12 or so. Rachel Carson (Silent Spring). A life of Dr. Albert Schweitzer (an author I don't recall). Reynolds Price, who made even "down-home" subjects seem poetic. Eric Hoffer's The True Believer. Gail Sheehy's Passages. Also, numerous essayists and journalists: Vermont Royster, William Raspberry, Ellen Goodman, Thomas Friedman, Leonard Pitts, Molly Ivins.

Obviously, I'd rather read the editorial pages and letters to the editor every night before bed than read somebody's made-up love story. To each his own; whatever they consider exciting. Granted, I'm the first to admit I don't choose to read seriously heavy subjects. Oh, yes, considering I majored in speech and drama, I once enjoyed reading plays.

(3) "Authors I Remember Well." Today, this week, it would be Ruth Reichl, because my answer to that is whoever wrote the last book I read. Ruth wrote Tender At The Bone in 1998. She was the restaurant critic for The New York Times, is now the editor of Gourmet. Just this weekend I ordered paperbacks of her next two books, some to give away to foodie friends of mine such as my nephew/godson, Chrish Peel, who sells wine in Raleigh. Yes, yes. Some books do make me crazy.

(4) "Preferred Styles of Writing." Anybody with an original turn of phrase, humorous, with a surprising twist.

Nothing pedantic or preachy. The humor hook grabs me much better than, say, the sarcasm of Rush Limbaugh.

(5) "Books That Have Changed Your Life." I would assume, the Holy Bible. The New Testament, anyway: Forgive. Turn the other cheek (I've never mastered that one). Love the unlovable (still working on that).

Gail Sheehy's Passages made an impact, helped me understand why men leave their wives. (Not always the wife's fault ... nor altogether his, either.) Eric Hoffer's The True Believer gave me an insight while watching political movements and their leaders, how alike — exactly alike — ideological extremists are, no matter what they stand for. They seem to stop thinking and start simply reacting to particular stimuli – words, phrases, flags, music, symbols – rather like dogs trained to salivate on cue. (My own observation, not Hoffer's.) Just last year, The Color of Water by James McBride. Some of these may not have changed my life so much as given it a certain direction. And I can't leave out Dr. Bernie Siegel's Humor and Healing.

I have my mother to blame for my addiction to newspapers and editorials. She read the Sunday funnies — "Little Orphan Annie," "Tarzan," "Dick Tracy," "Popeye," etc. — to me from age 3 on, and when I started correcting her mistakes, she said, "All right, little smarty. You read them to me."

"No, no," I insisted. "You read 'em to me."

"No."

"Yes."

Back and forth. After all, comics and cartoons are, basically, opinions and snapshot editorials, short-short stories popped open, served fast and fresh on the half shell. And slurped up.

Anyway, by age 5 or 6, I was reading the comics to her! Mamas amaze me. ✦

28

The Book That Changed My Life - *Magnificent Obsession* by Lloyd C. Douglas
(2008)

I can hear the modern-day journalism/creative writing teacher's voice ringing in my ears upon reading a line similar to, "We finally discovered a previously uninhabited park bench," in Lloyd C. Douglas's Magnificent Obsession. She or he would moan and propound (if you will), "Gee! Come off it. What's with all the puff and stuff? Why don't you simply and correctly say, 'We found an empty park bench?'"

Perhaps because I was born before the '70s.

40 years before.

In 1931.

However, this style of writing does seem dated today. In 1943, during World War II, when I was 12 years old, I read Little Women, Tom Sawyer, Huckleberry Finn, and Magnificent Obsession during the same three-month period. Thusly, if you will, my little pre-teen mind became aware of the Civil War and its portent, especially the saga of Huck and Jim, the slave that Huck tried to help escape.

But I was even more affected by Magnificent Obsession, which may seem a little quaint for today's readers. However, when I read it at that impressionable age, I thought the theory of old (actually, not so old, mid-fifties) Dr. Wayne Hudson was remarkable: to do a large favor, a really helpful action, for someone and insist they never tell anybody, and that they promise, when they are able, to help another person and never let it be known, because this builds up special strengths and powers within the giver that do not pervade that person if his generosity becomes known. Quaint, huh? That's what I said.

Needless to say, I have never been able to live up to his example. But after all, Dr. Hudson was a famous brain surgeon with money (and a worrisome daughter) and had more to give than I'll ever have. However, he died from drowning because his resuscitator had been borrowed across the lake to save the life of a rich, young, fratty-type, charming, tippling ne'er-do-well on his way to an early hell. Bobby Merrick lived, yes, and wonderful, generous, talented, verily-worshipped-by-so-many Doc Hudson died that day.

You know the rest if you've seen the 1954 film version with Rock Hudson and Jane Wyman: Robert Merrick discovered Hudson's secret, adopted it, got back into university and medical school and became able to, somewhat, take over the role of the magnanimous doctor.

Of course, there was romance tied in with the story; not today's usual offerings, but a high-minded romantic love story. However, that is not the point of this essay. In fact, I hardly remember, lo, these 65 years later, the love story. I was too intrigued by the giving-in-secret message.

Buddhists may refer to this as sending love into the universe.

29
Judge Junie on Prisons (20??)

My first husband, "Junie" Peel, graduated from Episcopal High School in Virginia and was Phi Beta Kappa at UNC. Between serving as a Navy officer in the Atlantic during World War II and doing active duty later with the Army in Korea, he graduated from UNC Law School in the same 1948 class as Bill Friday, Terry Sanford, Lindsey Warren, Jr., Judge Dickson Phillips, and E.K. Powe III. Junie went on to serve in the North Carolina House and was a State Senator when Governor Terry Sanford appointed him to the Superior Court bench (without asking him!). When I first asked him why he did not particularly enjoy his work as a judge, his answer was this:

"Lucia, when I am sitting up on that bench in my black robe and look down on the poor bastard standing in front of me, and realize that if he had my family and my education, and I had his family (if any) and his education (seg-regated schools at the time), I know that I'd be standing down there and he'd be sitting up here.

"How could I feel any sense of accomplishment from sending that fellow off to prison?" ✦

30

I Never Question the Tour Guide
(2008)

Well, hardly ever. I usually do not for fear of appearing a loud know-it-all, feigning ignorance by asking some little thing they might not have picked up in their vast previous travels abroad. (To show she knows the right questions to ask and that she's already been here before.)

However, I do recall asking four questions to three different guides on three separate trips, all in Africa. Apparently, I was so moved by their answers I remember them to this very day. More than I'd like.

The first was Cairo, Egypt. Except for our hotel and certain sites we were shown, we saw poverty, dust, dusty laundry hanging from every small apartment porch, dusty, hungry dogs wandering dusty streets, etc. Even the treasures in the world-famous museums needed dusting. So, I asked the pretty lady guide on the bus — a Christian, I recall — if these were the same people, the engineers, mathematicians, constructionists, who designed and created the Great Pyramids. She smiled. She said no and explained. That former civilization, that race, has been mixed many times over by others who came in, defeated them, exploited them and intermarried with them. Too bad the best warriors are not always the best nation builders.

In Kenya, I asked our guide (not in front of the group, never in front of others) if the men in the small poverty-stricken villages who fathered eight, ten, twelve children gave any thought as to how they would feed, clothe and educate their offspring. The guide, a highly educated native Kenyan, also smiled at my naiveté. No, in this society, he explained, a man's having many children was a sign of his manhood, his male prowess, his machismo. Education? Not an issue here. Clothes? Food? The female would provide, somehow. For the male to go hunting to provide food was a thing of the past. They kept a few goats, maybe a cow. Also, he added, you in the United States have Social Security. But in Kenya, their many children were social security. The assumption was that at least a few could survive and take care of the old man in his dotage. I would never have thought of that.

Questions three and four went to our guide another year, in Morocco. He often wore a brilliant yellow, flowing caftan and matching native headdress and beautiful, soft-leather, pointed slippers —also yellow, I suppose so we could not lose him in a crowded square or street. He stood out like neon. A polyglot, he was dark, handsome and already engaged to a blonde American school teacher he had met on one of his tours. I observed the poverty again, the beggars, the goat-herders, all exactly like the pictures we colored during our Sunday school lessons when I was a little girl. It all looked like a lesson about Jesus' time in the Holy Land two thousand years ago. No different. So, privately, I asked him why these good people had not moved into today's world.

He looked at me unblinking, right in the eye. I will never forget his answer. "Mrs. Powe, it's our religion. Our religion holds us back." Only since 9/11 have I come more to understand. If half the population is kept covered, hidden, uneducated, not allowed to drive, say, the other half of that society will hardly fly, grow or move on, either. Do children learn to love reading from their macho father? Maybe some do.

That afternoon our guide took us to a most exquisite mosque that overlooked the sea — possibly the largest in the world — constructed of lacy tall towers, with rounded tip tops pointing up into the late afternoon pink and gold clouds. The walls, floors, and ceilings were covered with millions — yes, millions — of colorful hand-made tiles. There were, however, no people there: no choir rehearsals, no soup kitchen, no clothes closet for the poor, no health classes for new mothers, and certainly not for unwed mothers.

(As an aside, forgive me, a couple of years ago, an unwed mother was scheduled to be stoned to death by Muslims in another area of Africa. Was the father of that infant scheduled to be stoned? Only the mother! Does it not take two to tango, even in Africa? Perhaps, like in the American

South, they have the same old expression, "She went out and got herself pregnant.")

Then I asked the fourth question. In this poor country, where did the money come from to build such a structure? It required millions of ... maybe not dollars, but money in some form. The answer: from Muslims in other countries, from all over the Islamic world. Ah, yes, black gold. Oil money. In effect, we oil-guzzling Americans largely paid for this mosque. In my mind's eye, I pictured the map showing the Muslim world, from Morocco to Afghanistan, sending oil money to build this Islamic cathedral. And I had to remind myself that Christians in Europe gathered money from the rich and poor to build their exquisite cathedrals. Even as poor, homeless beggars slept at night huddled up against the outer walls out of the cold wind. Inside, the warm bishops wore exquisite robes of satin, lace, and velvet — unlike Jesus Christ.

The mental map came back to me very recently when I saw a dark map of the world lit only by tiny white lights placed carefully in every location where a useful invention had been born in the last 2,000 years: the printing press, steam engine, gasoline engine, electricity, telephones, automobile, airplane, penicillin, computers.... Not hundreds but thousands of lights spread across the seven continents.

Except for the area from Morocco to Afghanistan. The Muslim world was shown in shocking, total darkness. Not a single light. Too bad the best warriors are not always the best nation-builders. ✦

31

The First Growl of the Dogs of War
(2009)

Needless to say, I never participated in active duty on a battlefield or warship. An only child, I had no brothers who served. My father was a diabetic. So I lived on the periphery of World War II, the Korean War, and the Vietnam War. I listened to the radio news, saved soap chips and kitchen grease, but never learned to knit socks or scarves or to wrap bandages.

However, my two husbands were very much in the thick of it, albeit before I met them. They were ten years older than I and played football against one another in prep school when they were 16. Later they were in the same class in college and law school and served together in the North Carolina General Assembly!

My first husband was on active duty in the Navy, chasing Nazi subs in the Atlantic, after he completed the Navy V-12 Program at UNC. No shots were fired at him, but he won the North Atlantic Cup for upchucking the most times on a four-hour watch one stormy night at sea. For three to four years he was seasick every time he left shore. (This before Dramamine!) He should not have been in the service at all, as he had a burst eardrum from diving, but he insisted his mother call her Washington friends and get him in any way. She did, much to her dismay. What if he'd been killed after she had pulled those strings? Her precious Junie: Phi Beta Kappa, a four-letter man in high school, witty, charming, bright.

Later; as a young lawyer in Williamston, he decided it would be a fine thing if the United States government built an indoor basketball court for the locals, himself included, in the form of an armory. The project was approved after many calls and letters to D.C., but now Junie had to recruit 75 or 80 boys to join the National Guard so the armory would be used for purposes more official than basketball! He even uncovered a CO, a retired Army Captain, who shortly thereafter suffered a heart attack. The D.C. people said, "Junie, now you're it."

"But I'm in the Navy Reserve," he replied.

They said easily, "We can fix that!" And they did.

From Navy blue to khaki to Korea. Picture this: His unit was the first in all North Carolina called to active duty, to Ft. Lee, Virginia. Junie's baby brother, whom he had recruited, was a junior at Virginia Episcopal School in Lynchburg and had to quit to report to Ft. Lee, which caused him to play catch-up for years to come. He graduated late from high school and went to UNC two or three years behind all his friends — and his girlfriend.

However, only two men from the Williamston unit were called to serve even more active duty on a hillside in South Korea for 18 months. You got it! The cook and the CO, Capt. Peel. To add insult to injury, one of the unit members who was left back at Ft. Lee went home every weekend and courted and married the captain's girlfriend. So much for the team-building properties of community basketball!

My second husband also served in World War II. E.K. Powe had been president of his freshman class and played football two seasons as a walk-on when he joined the army as a buck private. Soon he was sent to OCS and after only six weeks' training shipped out to France.

A pro football player named Al Blozis was in E.K.'s group that landed at Le Havre and caught the train to the Battle of the Bulge. Al was let off early where the alphabetical order required the "B's" to disembark. By the time E.K. Powe reached his post up near Alsace-Lorraine, his friend was already dead. E.K. was later wounded by shrapnel, sent to London for two weeks, then hustled back to the front, but he survived.

When my two husbands were in France and on the Atlantic during their early twenties, I was a pre-teen in junior high school. But I'll never forget when I heard the first growl of the dogs of war. In 1938 I was 7 years old in the second grade at Watts Street School in Durham. Every Thursday we were led to the Social Studies classroom, where for 45 minutes we studied a second-grade edition of My Weekly Reader and colored a picture from the lead story.

One week we colored the picture of a man in Europe named Adolph Hitler. He wore a mustache and held his arm straight out in front of him. The teacher then said we must be real quiet, "Shhhhh," as she turned on a radio for us to hear his voice.

When Hitler began to speak, my stomach clutched. Not understanding a word of German, I nevertheless heard hate, cruelty, pride, and sarcasm in that voice. Of course, at 7 years of age, I had no words for what I was feeling, an unnamable cringing, fear and dread. In guttural tones, he might have been saying, "We pure-blooded white Aryans have an obligation to spread our intelligence, physical prowess —look how often we are Olympic winners! — and strong leadership abilities over all Europe. We must cleanse our society of those who are not the chosen ones." (Chosen by whom?) "Achtung! The Fatherland uber alles! Heil!"

Then in response came, "Heil Hitler! Heil Hitler! Heil Hitler!" The frenzied, screaming was frightening — as if they had no brains, only vocal cords. How little did I know? Only later did I learn how Hitler used crowd psychology in renting a hall too small and hanging extra swastika flags, bright in color and design, a most powerful symbol of strength and power. He held back outside in order to arrive late so that the herd, followers — having listened to German marching bands pump out loud, pugilistic marches for an extra 45 minutes, and mostly standing for lack of seats, were frantic for der Fuhrer to arrive. And arrive he did. From the side, giant, heavy doors swung open, drums rolled, Hitler stepped through and shouted "Heil!"

No wonder he got such a wild-sounding reaction — and it was catching, from those excited supporters in the hall out to the listeners in many German homes. This is what we children heard on the radio, too, sitting in our little desks at Watts Street School in Durham, North Carolina. And you know the rest of it.

Sixty years later, I stepped into a Chinese shop on University Drive in Durham and heard another voice on the radio that gave me the same visceral reaction of repulsion. The words were in English but weren't really clear to me at first, though my gut did the same turnover, tightened right up. I felt as I had in 1938 at Watts Street School. I heard again a deep voice resonant with hate, ridicule, sarcasm, and accusations.

I asked the Asian woman behind the counter, "Whose voice is that on your radio?"

With a big smile, she said, "Oh, that is Lush Rimbaugh!"

P.S.: In 2004, Karl Rove arranged many of George W. Bush's political rallies to let in only card-carrying, cheering Republicans, though Bush was everybody's President. That was right here in Amerika! ✢

32

War: A Screed (Whatever That Is)
(2008)

Which war was a good war? Which was the bad?

The Peloponnesian Wars?

The Thirty Years War?

The American Revolutionary War?

The Napoleonic Wars?

The American Civil War? The "Civil" War? Why ever was it called the "Civil" War? There's nothing "civil" at all about fighting to defend the right to own slaves, even when you call that "states' rights" and "defending the Southern way of life" (buying and selling God's children of color). The Old Testament's Leviticus, the book of the Levites, states that owning slaves is fine if you don't purchase them locally but bring them from other countries. (Wow!) Is Leviticus's authority enough upon which to base our actions? The same book of the Old Testament says that homosexuality is a sin punishable by death; another faith today, Islam, agrees. (Neither recognizes that our race, color, and sex is established nine months before we are born, when the sperm hits the eggs, combining the DNA from the two parents.)

Again, which war? World War I? World War II? The Korean conflict? Tell me again why our boys (and my first husband) were in Korea. The United States owned neither North nor South Korea, and neither country had attacked us.

The Vietnam War? 'Nam? Same there, we owned neither North nor South. Despite that, we lost over 50,000 men! (Was Halliburton, Dick Cheney's company, in business then?) Oh, yes, according to the Domino Theory we were "containing" communism, preventing a cascade that could only end with the final domino resting upon a piling of the Golden Gate Bridge.

Could we not have dealt with the North Vietnamese as we did with the U.S.S.R.? We did not attack them. We did what we do best: we give more citizens a good life with our democratic system of capitalism, each man in his own boat, a system in which all boats can rise. Time and its own dysfunctional governmental and economic systems took care of Soviet Russia. The nation's leaders in Moscow couldn't get enough typewriters and enough electricity to their far-flung provinces to do the government's work, so it caved.

Communist Cuba's citizens still risk life, limb and drowning to escape their government and try to get to our land. Granted, Cuba's former Batista government needed serious improvement. But imagine what capitalism would have made of Cuba in the last half-century since Fidel Castro took over as Cuba's president: Cuba might have become a most beautiful, successful world resort!

We were told that our wars to "contain" communism in Korea, Cuba, and Vietnam were ideological wars – our ideas versus their ideas. But were they "logical" wars?

Now, we are told that we are containing terrorism ... or the spread of Jihad, radical Islam. First, in 2002, we were told we were defending ourselves from future attacks by atomic weapons. Then we were told we were destroying a despotic dictator, Saddam Hussein. How about the other dozens of despotic leaders, some closer to home and thus, presumably, more threatening to our country? Why aren't we taking them on, too? Then we're told we're "spreading democracy." What is the truth about why we occupied Iraq?

Now, this is truly dear, our desire to teach our way of freedom to a nation that does not have a tradition of democracy in its history or secular culture or religion. That is good, but is it realistic?

Our word and concept of democracy came down to us from the Greek language, from the word demos, meaning "the people." The language spoken by the Iraqis does not derive from the Greek, but from the East Semitic Akkadian around 2000 B. C. and later from Arabic, the lingua franca today. Iraq has given laws and great lawgivers, but no ideal or history of citizenship, with a senate or legislature elected by the people, as in ancient Greece and Rome, the two cultures that shaped our own European roots. Instead, Iraqi laws were handed down by their rulers from a totally different history.

Could the cause of the problem be ... testosterone? Because of this hormone, fighting, and wars – none of them "good" – have gone on since the beginning of time, since the males of the species stood up on their hind legs and began fighting with tools instead of teeth and claws. Mother Nature, perhaps fortunately so, granted testosterone to the male so he might protect himself, his mate, his offspring and cave, and later his land, fields, and property. No wars have been led by females, Joan of Arc excepted. (And she was burned at the stake!) Of course, testosterone enabled the male to create and continue the human race.

Women, if allowed to govern, might follow an inherently different style. Women might come together to talk it all over first — then talk it to death! That's where the death would come in, perhaps in the kitchen before sharing recipes. I do believe that women would go much farther in negotiations to prevent all-out war, because they do not want to send their baby boys, born of their wombs, nursed at their breasts, off to some foreign field to murder, to kill other baby boys (still and always "babies" in their mothers' minds) and to be killed themselves. Do our mothers love their baby males more than their war-mongering fathers do?

Just askin'. ✛

33

Ask a Lemming
(2009)

Lemming - n (Norw) Any of several small short-tailed, furry-footed rodents ... of circumpolar distribution that are notable for recurrent mass migrations ... which often continue into the sea where vast numbers are drowned. — Webster Seventh New Collegiate Dictionary (1965)

Our high-school biology teacher, when asked why lemmings performed this self-destructive maneuver, could only offer the assumption that they somehow received a signal that their environment would only support a limited number and for their breed to continue, they had to move out of the way; in effect, to make room for future generations. Was I satisfied with that answer at the time? Probably not. And I still ponder it at times. Maybe once a year.

However, when we look at the human animal, now standing on his hind legs, able to look up and out more than to the ground, we do wonder what makes him so determined, every generation or so, to destroy other humans and in the process destroy himself or many of his own group. We humans so quickly forget the horrors of war and seem to believe, like teenagers, that we are invincible; others may die, but we'll come home safely to flags a'waving.

Leaders have little trouble drumming up a desire to go to war. Just turn a sufficient number of men against other men for any number of reasons — race, retaliation, territory — and outcome the flags, bugles, uniforms, and guns.

If an additional reason is ever needed, R-E-L-I-G-I-O-N is always ready and waiting: We must kill Them in the name of God — our God — before They kill Us in the name of their god. "Praise Allah," shouts the Muslim before he slices off the head of the journalist, on television. I am tempted to ask an extremist Muslim that if Allah made him, who made us? If Allah made us all, does He want his children to destroy one another? In His name?

"Onward Christian Soldiers, marching as to war, with the cross of Jesus, going on before. Like a mighty army...."

In so many words, this is what the "Christian" soldiers of the crusades sang on the way to the land of the birth of Jesus to kill the infidels, discover the silver chalice and bring it home to jolly old England. What they really did was kill the men, rape the women, burn the mosques and bring home gold, much of which can be seen in castles and museums throughout Europe today. Can we even imagine how many people have been killed in the name of sweet Jesus? The same man that exhorted us to, that's right, "love one another." Three simple words. He did not say, "Love one another if they are just like you," or "Love one another if they are [white, straight, clean, etc]."

If the crusades weren't bad enough, then came the Spanish Inquisition, when Catholic Monarchs used the church as an excuse to kill, burn and hang. The Catholics were killing the Protestants in Spain, and in England, the church led the government to kill the Catholics; some of this bad feeling lingers even today in Ireland. The irony here is, both sides claim to believe in Jesus. What in Christ's name — and I do not mean that to be disrespectful — are they fighting about?

Point being, it begins to appear obvious that the male of the species has a need — a deep need — to fight. Is it to prove his manhood? Is it the testosterone? Testosterone was given by mother nature, no doubt, so the male could fight off enemies (thieves, wild animals), kill animals for food and eventually play a game of football. Could more worldwide male sports, using up all that testosterone, prevent wars?

We can wonder what would happen if women were allowed to dominate the peace table. Rather than threaten war with knives, hatchets, swords, bullets, and bombs, like the males, would the ladies not just talk it over? "How can we work this out? After all, I don't want my little boy out there killing your boy, nor want your boy to kill my boy. That is not why I gave birth, suckled, hugged and loved him: to prepare him to be a murderer, a killer, a soldier carefully trained to kill your son."

Defense? Ah, yes. We must always be ready to defend ourselves. And while we're at it, we'll hire a scientist like Oppenheimer to create an atomic bomb. That'll show 'em who has more testosterone.

"We're gonna git 'em, dead or alive." Cowboys and Indians. Meet 'em at the pass and kill 'em all dead. Little American boys make guns from sticks at 2, 3 and 4 years old, or would except their fathers have already given them guns in holsters to play "bang, bang, you're dead." America features more gun-deaths per population than any other country on the planet, by far. Some voters want a gun in every hand.

"As the twig is bent ...."

Do humans, like the lemmings, have a self-destructive hormone? A built-in death-wish, an angel of death that leads us to glorify war, fighting, killing?

Perhaps the Bible is right, "There will be wars and rumors of wars ..."

One more example: Thousands of men fought for "the southern way of life," meaning the states' rights to buy and sell slaves. Approximately one-half of one percent of Southerners actually owned slaves. Some slave-owners sent their sons to England to avoid fighting. Others hired men to take their place, or even sent their slaves to fight! More men died in that war than the U.S. lost in both World War I and World War II combined! Why would thousands of non-slave-owners agree to leave home, fight and die so that so few of their number could own slaves? Especially since, in 1861, the sons of any man who owned more than 25 slaves did not have to go to war! Did they truly love the thrill of fighting so much? Is that the meaning of "Blood Sport?"

Hey, could it be blamed on testosterone? Hmm…? ✦

34

That Box in My Brain
(2017)

That special box in the brain where I've always stored names is apparently becoming too stuffed so that I cannot ... pull ... one ... out ... anytime I want to — or need to! Oh. My. God! (I mean, "Gosh!")

Granted, it's worse now I'm in my eighties, but don't tell me it's just age! One remedy is to run down the alphabet — mentally, not physically. That often helps, but not always. Fortunately, I live in the South, where we can call everybody "Darlin'" or "Hon'" or "Sugar." Thank you, Lord!

Not having a talent for recalling names, how did I ever manage to work as a "stringer" for the News & Observer newspaper, covering stories in northeastern North Carolina, from Bath and Manteo on the coast, inland to Elizabeth City, Edenton, Greenville, Rocky Mount, and Wilson? And the N&O even paid me! — 11 cents an inch! Wow! ✦

35

The Beauty Queen Comes to Durham
(1994)

In the hot summer of 1962, the Durham Junior Chamber of Commerce hosted the statewide Miss North Carolina Pageant at the venerable Durham High School. The Jaycees and the whole city rolled out the red carpet for the influx of fifty or more hometown winners, their chaperones, parents, friends, families, hairdressers, musical accompanists, and boyfriends. A typically Southern circus had rolled into town and every hotel, motel, and restaurant was filled; the eyes of the business community sparkled with dollar signs. Exactly what the Jaycees wanted, right?

The contestants that year, however, did not lodge at hotels. They and their chaperones were carefully placed in fifty private homes.

Chaperone. That was my role that sunny summer weekend from Wednesday 'til Sunday. I was married to Judge Junie Peel in Williamston, Martin County, and the beautiful, athletic, musical, exceptional young lady who had been named Miss Martin County was his third cousin.

(You read that right: It's likely only Southerners have or acknowledge third cousins.)

Junie had served as president of the Williamston Jaycees as a young attorney before he was elected to the state Senate, where he became a friend of Durham attorney Nick Galiafanakis. Consequently, the Jaycees decided that I, Junie's wife, had an obligation to attend our Martin County Queen, Blanche Hodges Manning, to the big city of Durham for the statewide event.

"I don't mind going," I told them, "but I have two little girls at home."

"Not to worry," said their new president. "Our wives will keep your children while you are in Durham with 'Blanchy-Boo'?"

They had it all arranged before they spoke to me.

But how does one say "No" to a girl loved by everyone in our town of 5,000, especially one known to all as "Blanchy-Boo"?

For starters, she was a tall, 5'9" basketball captain with black, wavy hair; large, expressive eyes; a wide, sincere smile; beautiful teeth; and the most unselfconscious, unassuming "Manning" manner that ever charmed a teacher, boyfriend, child or neighbor. Furthermore, she could sing and play the piano. She had grown up with a horse in her backyard and not only trained but talked to horses and dogs. Cross my heart. I saw her in action. She knew their language and could read their minds. But that's another story.

Blanche taught my daughter Sydney to ride and "show" English saddle and even to jump. Hear that? Taught my shy child how to take a horse over the top of a hurdle!

Upon arriving in Durham, each contestant and chaperone were introduced to their Jaycee escort, who would chauffeur the two all weekend to official events. There were no unofficial events. Every moment was planned. Rehearsal, luncheon, rehearsal, tea, shop, meet the press, try to sneak a nap. Too excited to sleep. Don't let the hometown down.

With the orchestra Blanche rehearsed her talent number, "Wouldn't It Be Loverly," from the Broadway show My Fair Lady. They loved her. We were staying in Trinity Park, guests of a lovely widow lady whose name I cannot recall. After all, this was more than forty years ago! Our driver apologized for our being in a fairly small home.

"It's wonderful," declared Blanche. "We love Mrs. 'Smith.' She could not be nicer, and our room is perfect."

He also mentioned with a twinkle in his eye that he had been asked to approach another widow lady in a very large house with four(!) empty bedrooms plus her own. She had hemmed and hawed and finally said she was so sorry but her yard man was coming that weekend. Our driver said it was all he could do not to ask if the yard man intended to stay overnight. However, he resisted and merely thanked her. He had perfect manners.

Blanche had a great laugh. "Hey, don't hold that against her! Maybe she thought we'd steal the silver."

Funny the things we remember forty years later — especially when we can't even remember our hostess's name.

While in Durham we shopped at Montaldo's and Baldwin's (both now closed). We bought safety pins and thread at the S.H. Kress store on Main Street. They say we cannot remember smells. Well, I beg their pardon. I still recall the smell of Kress's: a combination of roasted peanuts in oil, slightly rancid popcorn, "Midnight" cologne, candies under glass, chocolate malt balls and candy corn. I did not purchase the cologne in the midnight-blue and silver bottle.

Blanche had hoped to go to a Durham Bulls baseball game but there was no time. She later married Gaylord Perry of Williamston, the world-famous southpaw who pitched major-league baseball until he was 45 years old! Whose pitching arm (or legs, for that matter) could hold up for 27 years? Only Gaylord's.

Blanche and I visited McDonald's 74 Drugstore on Ninth Street and also passed E.K. Powe Elementary School. I remember thinking, "What an odd name for a school! Poe spelled P-O-W-E." Did it occur to me that forty years later I would find myself married to E.K. Powe and living in Durham? Of course not.

The final night arrived. Blanche looked exquisite, some said like a taller Jackie Kennedy. Her Eliza Dolittle costume was perfect. Her song delighted everybody. She did not win. Did this bother Blanche? Not a whit. She had a grand time and enjoyed every minute of it. Perhaps it was her athletic experiences — golf, tennis, and basketball —

that had taught her to take losing and winning with equal grace. Or perhaps it was just her "raising" as a Manning.

But a funny thing happened on the way to the forum, uh, pageant. Our driver said, "Oh, damn. I just missed the turn. Lessee, how am I going to get back onto Gregson?" Durham High School was and is across Duke Street from large tobacco-curing warehouses, and Gregson runs from north to south just behind the school.

"You're fine," said Blanche. "Just turn left up here a block, then right a block, then left again to Duke Street."

He almost wrecked the car. "Blanche," he gasped and stared at her. "How do you know how to get around Durham?"

I personally preferred he kept his eyes on the road.

"Oh, didn't I tell you? I'm a rising junior at Duke. I've already spent two years in Durham. My daddy was a Dukie too. He couldn't wait to get me up here."

He shook his head trying to absorb this new information about her, his charge, that she had failed to mention. So, of course, I could not resist sharing that I also had lived two years in Durham, on Gregson Street in 1937 and 1938 when I was in the first and second grades at Watts Street School. My teacher was Miss Pridgen, the very woman Frances Gray Patton wrote about in Good Morning, Miss Dove, the book and the movie. I still have my report cards somewhere, signed by Miss Pridgen and the principal, Miss Lilly. I remember seeing live productions of Peter Pan and Jack and the Beanstalk at the Carolina Theater and visiting Duke Gardens on Sunday afternoons with my parents.

Though Blanche was 12 years younger than I, she treated me more like a sister than a chaperone, and vice versa. We often laughed later about our big trip to Durham as guests of the Junior Chamber of Commerce — a high ol' time and not in the modem sense of the word. We were both high on the fun and hospitality of everyone we met.

This story might be more amusing, perhaps, if I had portrayed Blanche (and that nickname!) as a country-girl-come-to-town, wide-eyed and simple. But that was not Blanche. In fact, our Jaycee escort might have been even more impressed had he known she spent the summer before, her debutante summer, in New York City studying voice and piano. Stepping into the spotlight in a long white gown was not new to her, as she had come home from New York the previous August to be presented at the North Carolina debutante ball in Raleigh.

While in New York she had attended every New York Giants baseball game she could manage. Remember, she later married Mister Baseball, Gaylord Perry. They had four children, all good horsemen. She trained them for both English and Western saddle. They were winning ribbons in shows at home while their father was away winning big-league pennants. A family of winners. How strange it is that I am now enjoying life in Durham, and Blanche ...

Blanche is not living at all.

The day after her first grandchild was born, our Blanchy-Boo was killed by a drunken driver.

I haven't yet gotten over it.

She left warm, delicious memories as soul-soothing as her biscuits. Obviously, one of my favorite memories was our visit to Durham in 1962. I still remember brick warehouses on Duke Street across from the high school shimmering in the golden glow of late afternoon sunshine. The sweet smell of tobacco coming from inside, as rich to the nose as dark, warm chocolate. And I see Blanche's broad, beautiful smile as she enjoyed every minute of our visit in Durham that long weekend of the pageant. ✦

36

My Friend Gwen
(1999)

Answer machine message, December 2, 1998: "Lucia, We'll pick you up at 10:30 tomorrow, Thursday, to ride together to Stelle's luncheon in Burlington. Let me know if you get this message, hear? Bye now."

That was Lucille Jones's voice. Lucille, wife of beloved pediatric and adolescent psychiatrist Dr. Dave Jones. And he did love children. They had seven.

I, in turn, left a strange, for me, message, not the usual, "Hey, great, thank you. I'll be ready." Instead, I heard myself say, "Thank you so much, Lucille. Actually, I'll be needing my own car. But I'll see you there, okay?" I didn't explain why I needed to take my own car. I did not know why I needed to drive alone. Something told me, "Drive your own car."

Toward the end of Stelle's most lovely luncheon at the Burlington Country Club the next day, Donnie Strayhorn slipped over to my table and whispered that Bill Entwistle, Gwen's husband in Winston-Salem, had died at his desk at home of a heart attack sometime after she had ridden off to Burlington with her friends. "We who drove her over here have been instructed to tell Stelle, you and her other friends here not to tell Gwen. Her minister and her doctor insist on breaking it to her when she comes home."

Then I knew.

"I'm following you to Winston-Salem," I told her. Donnie said, "Fine, but don't let Gwen see your car, hear? Stay far back, out of sight, okay?" I asked her how she and the others in the car were going to handle this all the way home. Donnie just shook her head.

Much later, Gwen told me it had been the weirdest time, the ride home when she would say something funny, nobody laughed.

I followed along back a distance and pulled up into the drive behind their car and was there when the minister came out to the car to lead Gwen into the house. I phoned my husband, E.K., that I was staying overnight to help answer the door, answer the phone, make coffee, just to "be there."

When I arrived back in Durham the next afternoon on Friday, a message was on the answering machine that Gwen, the family, and the minister were counting on me to sing Bill's favorite hymn, "Amazing Grace," as a solo at the funeral service Saturday afternoon. The program had already gone to print.

We surely want to "do" for our friends, but how in heaven's name could I sing, remember the words, not choke or cry at a close friend's funeral? They just weren't thinking! E.K. kept assuring me on the drive over Saturday afternoon that, of course, I could do it. I lifted a little prayer, a big one, actually, and "Amazing Grace" amazed me again. The song came off passing well as far as I recall. Anyway, E.K. was not embarrassed.

Truth be known, Gwen has so many dozens of friends and we all knew she would do anything she could for us, embarrassing or not. She would come through for us, weather and her health permitting. She lifts us up. She steps into our rooms with her bright, positive smile and the room rises two, three inches. She never criticizes or complains. She praises. She sees only the best in you ... and then some. Naturally, her friends and her children try to live up to the vision she has for us. Clearly, her faith lifts her up and she spreads joy from her Source, but she never tries to save your soul or push her faith onto others. Actually, she did give me a copy, as a house gift, of Streams in the Desert, written by a woman, L.S. Cowman, in 1925, a book of daily devotions. I submit that I do not read one every day as I believe Gwen does. One, for instance, begins, "I will cause you to ride on the heights of the land" (Isaiah 58: 14). Cowman's commentary begins, "One of the first rules of aerodynamics is that flying into the wind increases altitude." See what I mean?

Gwen's life has not been easy. Her mother died when she was a toddler. Her father later married a lady who reared Gwen and her siblings in a circle of love. After graduating from UNC Gwen received her Master's in Education from the University of Virginia, taught, married, reared five outstanding children, sold real estate, and has been married now three times and has survived the deaths of all three husbands.

Bill Entwistle was her second husband. She nursed the last, the third gentleman, who was so sick she nearly ruined her own health, barely surviving the ordeal. She had to be hospitalized and was given a pacemaker.

When Gwen's third husband died, a Chapel Hill lady called me offering a ride to the funeral; she was a delightful person whom I'd never met. She said Gwen stopped her jogging by the road one day and said she knew such a person of her (our) age, must be special to be out jogging that time of day. They were great friends ever since. Can't you see Gwen pulling her car to a stop beside the road, rolling down the window and calling her over – a stranger?

Gwen never limits her friends to one or two specific cliques. She never sees people through a screen of prestige or money, whether they are "in" or "out," old, young or popular. I met her first when we were both widows at a gala in Wilmington and she instantly, out of nowhere, invited me to her 60th birthday party at a friend's house in Chapel Hill two days later. Through her, I've met so many delightful people, some of whom sustain me today.

She "set me up" with Tom Davis, a Winston-Salem widower who had founded Piedmont Airlines, now US

Air, in the late '30s. We all had fun together. She was disappointed when I married E.K. — until she met him, and of course, she loved and admired him also.

Gwen simply wants everyone she touches to be happy, and her calling, clearly, is to make just that happen.

Aren't I the lucky one?

Postscript, 2017: Gwen went to her great reward in 2013. ✦

37

The Only Tibetan Monk I Know
(2008)

I have the privilege of knowing a tall, slender Tibetan monk – self-contained, reserved, and holy in demeanor and bearing. Every day I see him in saffron robes, with a shaved head, dusky complexion, long, slim, gentle hands, and kind brown eyes. He walks into my house like an Indian brave enters the woods, gliding soundlessly across a boundary I do not see and into my world.

Actually, Nathaniel Dickerson is not Tibetan. And he's not Indian. He is a light-complexioned African-American man from Durham, North Carolina. And he does not wear holy robes but has the bearing of a kind, selfless priest in his daily dress, the white jacket of a professional, highly trained nurse. I am quite sure, for example, that Nathaniel has never rudely awakened a patient by careless, heavy footsteps. And his ways are indeed holy, for his own reasons and his patients', as he greatly respects his calling and thus gives much more than is required.

When my husband's Parkinson's condition continued to deteriorate, we received numerous calls from his old friend and legal client, Kenan Rand, to consider hiring his own former nurse, Nathaniel Dickerson. Kenan felt his gentle nature and many years of experience would be good for E.K.

Kenan was correct.

When Nathaniel steps through the front door mild and smiling, both E.K. and I feel our blood pressure sliding down as surely as it does, for instance, when we sit together and listen to Johann Pachelbel's Baroque and 18th-century music, the peaceful classical music that lowers the blood pressure of surgical patients and often results in up to 50 percent less blood loss during invasive surgery.

Nathaniel is a widower, ageless, perhaps 77 years old, accepting, tolerant, soft-spoken. When he makes a suggestion concerning E.K.'s medical treatment, he does it wisely and only for E.K.'s well-being, never for his own ego. He was admired so as a nurse's aide at UNC Hospitals that they offered him a scholarship for further professional training as a practical nurse.

In the 1950s and '60s, for twelve or more years, Nathaniel was the personal attendant to poet Ezra Pound at St. Elizabeth's Hospital, a mental institution outside Washington, D.C. Pound, convicted of treason for his broadcasts from Fascist Italy during the Second World War, was declared mentally ill and placed in an asylum rather than sent to prison where he would have been eaten alive for being a traitor. Nathaniel calls Pound's sentencing to St. Elizabeth's "going to the White House rather than the Big House." He enjoyed those years in Washington and said the dinner parties given by Pound were very lively when Robert Frost and other poets came to visit with their mentor.

Today Nathaniel arrives at my house carrying a small black bag under his arm. It looks like an old-fashioned doctor's kit but is, in fact, a fine set of manicure equipment. Without even asking, he gives E.K. a manicure and pedicure and refuses extra pay. Likewise, he will not accept payment for the special shampoo he prefers to use for his patients.

This fine man makes my husband's outings so much more pleasant, partly because of his assistance with the wheelchair and his helping me get E.K. into and out of the car, but also for the pleasure Nathaniel appears to derive from these ventures, whether to a UNC basketball game or to a literary evening at Burnside Plantation honoring North Carolina authors.

The detailed stories Nathaniel tells me of his years assisting Ezra Pound, and later Jimmy Hoffa, prove he is an observant man; he recalls conversations he has heard among our friends about politics, news, race relations, books, and music. He openly discusses these matters with me, gives me his opinions, and I am flattered that Nathaniel trusts me and takes my opinions seriously, too, just as he did the opinions of Robert Frost, John Steinbeck,

William Faulkner and other authors he met through Ezra Pound.

But as with any life, there is tragedy in it. The tragedy in Nathaniel's life is that he was not born into circumstances that would have allowed him to attend medical school. We can only imagine the thousands of patients who would have been so fortunate to have had him, a surgeon, come to them just before surgery, take both hands in his, smile gently, mildly, and say, "Everything is going to be all right." These words and Dr. Nathaniel's demeanor alone might lower their blood pressure and make even the most difficult procedure a success and allow less blood to be lost by those privileged patients. ✢

38

Fan
(2009)

Bam, bam, knock, knock, bam! Fan's deck of cards she was shuffling for her game of Solitaire flew up in the air and landed all over the floor. Jumping up, she and her cook, Bea Balance, both ran to the front door, tore it open and discovered three excited, panicky, breathless African-American children.

"Miz Fannie Myrt, hurry, you gotta come with us. Quick. Bymanishus is dayud."

"How do you know?" She nearly shouted, her hand over her heart.

"We saw him through his window. His doors was locked. He was laid out on the floor fronta' his sofa ... dayud as a doornail."

The house painter had borrowed her car, and she could not run with them six blocks, so she called the Police Chief, Howard Griffin. When he came back later, hat in hand, he told her Bymanishus was not dead. Just passed-out drunk.

"What a relief! Gracious. How did you get in?"

"Ma'am, we had to take out a gun and shoot the lock to bust in there. The neighbors went wild, running every whicher way, like bees roaring out of a hive ... Mis' Fannie Myrt, tell me why those chirrun' came running to you and didn't call us in the first place."

"Darlin', I have no idea." She smiled, shrugging.

"By the way, what kinda' name is Bymanishus?" he asked. Now, Fan laughed out loud.

"Oh, yes. After I called him that for ten years — he's our yard man, you know — my daughter-in-law told me that he had told her on the first day here I had asked him what people called him and when he said, 'by my initials,' before he could get out 'J.D.,' I had burst in and said, 'Wonderful. Like that old Greek philosopher, Dionysius.' And I was so pleased with myself. He was too new and embarrassed to correct me, nor ever after. Now everybody calls him Bymani... but, look here. Won't you step in and have a glass of iced tea?"

Chief Griffin said, "Thanks," but explained he had to get back downtown.

✦✦✦

That lady was my first mother-in-law, Frances Myrtle Manning Peel. She hated her nickname, "Fannie Myrt." When her son, Elbert Sidney Peel, Jr. and I tried to name any of our four daughters for her, she strongly objected, so we let her name them all — sort of. Fannie Myrt was 5'9" tall, unaffected, smoked cigarettes for far too many years, loved to read, cared little for clothes, jewelry, finery, bric-a-brac, yet had very good taste in both "things" and people. She recognized "quality" in white and black, rich and poor, in furniture and antiques. Her style of arranging flowers, rather than the formal "S" curve, was her own "stick-and-poke" style. Beautiful, nevertheless. Her hair was almost white at age 33. She never dyed it, of course.

She grew up in Williamston, North Carolina, where her father, William Christian Manning, owned several small area newspapers, the local telephone company, and the electric power company. During the Depression in the '30s, he was forced to sell the phone company to Carolina Telephone and Telegraph and the power company to Virginia Electric Power Company, known later as VEPCO. As a young wife and mother, before she and Mr. Elbert built their own house after he returned home from World War I and had finished law school at the University of North Carolina, they lived in the old Manning family home with her parents. Her mother helped raise Elbert Jr. ("Junie"), my future husband. Fannie Myrt's father, "Mr. Crish," had her down at the newspaper helping him, and she was also in charge of all the telephone operators at the phone company. Obviously, she was quite capable.

Harking back to her courting days when she was a student at Atlantic Christian College (now Barton) in Wilson, N.C., she had finally managed to be known as "Fan," rather than "Fannie Myrt." When Elbert drove over from Greenville, where he was a 19-year-old(!) principal of the high school (he had entered UNC-Chapel Hill at 15 and graduated Phi Beta Kappa four years later), he called up the stairs of the ladies' dorm, "Fannie Myrt!" And she was so mad she almost refused to come down for their date. A "date" translated as sitting in the parlor with other couples in the company of a chaperone. Someone would play the piano and they might sing a wild song ... like "My Wild Irish Rose."

Fan was known as a "soft touch." Needy people showed up at her back door often and never left disappointed: food, clothes, even money for bus tickets to Wilson to "grandma's funeral" (even when she knew the same "granny" had already died six times).

She summered for thirty years or more at the Old Arlington Hotel at Nags Head, built of gray weathered cedar siding, porches all 'round, now washed into the sea. Mr. Elbert only drove down on weekends, as he'd rather practice law in Martin County than rock on a porch at the beach. Boring. Not for Fan. They had lent money to the couple to buy the hotel, so she felt a tad of responsibility and played unofficial hostess, arranging dune grass, shells, and cattails in large vases in the lobby, and inviting new guests to have a snappy bourbon and "branch" on the porch before dinner. The hotel had no bar.

Back home, she taught a challenging Sunday School class; devoured the Sunday New York Times, which arrived on Tuesday; and ordered linens from the January "White Sales," only sheets with 400-count cotton per inch. Ordered her granddaughters hand-smocked frocks from Best & Co., now defunct. "Smock" their dresses herself? Well ... no. However, during tax season, she had several dozen clients for whom she prepared tax returns, first at

Peel and Peel law office, 'til her husband ran her home. Too little space for her clients and his. So, she worked with them at her dining room table, shoving the candelabra aside. Tah da!

As a girl of 12 or so, she accompanied her mother, Mrs. Manning, to the country to help a sick, bed-ridden mother with an alcoholic husband and children. Fan and her mom would wash all their clothes in the black wash pot over a fire in the yard, hang them to dry, cook a pot of soup over a wood stove in the kitchen, and — are you ready? — pick the nits from the kids' hair.

Even so, later, the Junior League and the Terpsichorean Club of Raleigh tapped Fan to send up the debutantes from the area to be presented at North Carolina's Annual Deb Ball.

That image always amused me: unpretentious Fannie Myrt for years selecting debutantes. If she had daughters, no doubt, she would have refused, but she had only boys, my future husband, and his younger brother. ✦

39

Another Heartbeat in the House
(2012)

Ten months after my husband, E.K. Powe, passed away, my second daughter Mimi's family apparently decided I needed another heartbeat in the house; someone, something, to talk to — my being a bit of a "talkie" grandma.

So, what did they do? They gave me one of their two cats — the newest one (11 years old). On Halloween day of 2000, the family was enjoying lunch on their screened-in back porch in Forest Hills in Durham when a feral (abandoned) kitty "adopted" the family, even though they already had a cat. She would not leave them even when told, "Scat, cat. Please go away." When the family tried to walk around the block together, the kitty ran after them. All the way out and back home again.

Finally, giving in, they took her in and my granddaughter Lily named her "Punkin," short for "Pumpkin" (Halloween, remember?), though she was not orange. Oh no, Punkin is coal-black all over, except for a white streak on her nose, white neck, chest, stomach, and four exquisitely white pretty paws.

Who would have thought our God was such an artist to create such a delightfully designed creature? Not to mention the black-and-white zebras!

When they presented Punkin to me, 11 years later, I was 81 years old and had never heard the expression "tuxedo cat." Have you? Well, I was in the minority. Everybody knew what a tuxedo cat is, and now I owned one. Lily was 11 years old when the baby kitty showed up and grandson Tom, also at the table, was 13, and approved the addition of this new family pet. The family could picture me talking to my new companion.

"Punkin, what time do you want your breakfast?"

"Neeowww."

"Coming right up! Punkin, did you hear the doorbell ring?"

"Neooooow. You can answer it yourself, ol' girl." ✦

40

Ruby Therapy or Romper Room to KidzNotes
(2017)

Could observing one, even one, of the younger creatures of the human species grow, mature, learn, laugh and charm be one of the most beautiful, compelling, rewarding experiences we older humans ever enjoy? Grandma Powe submits that it is!

As I've been permitted to observe this miracle through four daughters and four (plus six step-) grandchildren, I can attest to the therapeutic properties of said experience.

To those special grandchildren I hereby express my gratitude: Lily Elkins, Stewart Woodside, Joey Woodside and the most recent, Ruby Solow.

This "fetish" (weakness?) of mine may have begun with my most favorite job — no, not just a "job," but a five-day-a-week party, celebration, you name it, of teaching —

on live television with CBS station WNCT in Greenville, North Carolina, where I "taught" Romper Room as "Miss Lucia" in the 1950s. Yours truly was laughing all the while with six adorable, "ruly" (as in, "not unruly") children, three boys and three girls, playing games, playing musical instruments (drums, horns, etc.), singing songs and telling stories (and slipping in a few commercials — eek! — but the station had to make a living), 'til all a'sudden the bell rang and it was over! Five daze a week. Such a privilege!

Imagine getting paid to do that!

Then marriage, the four ah-may-zing daughters, directing three choirs, teaching Sunday school, directing four Girl Scout troops (not all the same year), teaching ballet and art, performing in summer theatre, serving on boards, bringing the North Carolina Symphony to Martin County and teaching in the public schools...

Then, however, my sweet, brilliant (Phi Beta Kappa) husband, Judge Elbert ("Junie") Peel, died at age 62 of pancreatic cancer. (Not lung cancer, as neither of us had ever smoked.)

Many years later, I was living in Durham with my second husband, E.K. Powe. On July 6, 2008, he and I were watching 60 Minutes. (Why can I recall that date and so few others? And names escape me regularly.) E.K. was in his wheelchair with Parkinson's (he had played walk-on hoofball —I mean, football — at UNC) and could not walk, talk or see (except a bit), but he could hear, thus the television. The program that night featured a story on "El Sistema" ("The System"), a method of helping underprivileged children succeed in school by teaching them to play classical music. It had been founded in Caracas, Venezuela, some 45 years earlier by Dr. José Antonio Abreu — not an M.D., but an economist serving in the Venezuelan Senate who was also a musician.

So just what has El Sistema accomplished? It started at inner-city schools with many at-risk children, 70 or 80 percent of whom have no father figure in their lives. They may have a father in prison, but they have no daddy to pull them up on his lap and read to them; they may never even see a man reading a book or newspaper! Their moms are overwhelmed, struggling to play both parenting roles while feeding, housing and supporting them. Sadly, many are headed for prison from the day they are born.

Dr. Abreu began teaching basic violin to eleven under-privileged children in an abandoned garage in Caracas. In a few years, he and others were training hundreds, perhaps thousands, of children across Venezuela in cities, country, and suburbs. He also made a connection with the New England Conservatory of Music in Boston. One of his students who was featured on the 60 Minutes program, Gustavo Dudamel, became director of the Los Angeles Symphony — at age 27! Now Dudamel, nicknamed "the Dude," tours the planet with the Symphony and as guest director of other world-famous orchestras. (Grandma Powe has enjoyed five live concerts he directed, four in Los Angeles and one in Rome with the Italian national orchestra; she forgets the name but remembers the experience.)

Sooo... back to 60 Minutes. Under various names ("The Program," "Music First," "All Together Now"), El

Sistema had already spread all over the Americas and around the world but had not yet reached the Southern United States. E.K heard me mumble, "Wouldn't it be nice to have that in Durham?"

He could barely talk but he whispered, "Lucia, why don't you start it?"

Laughing, I replied, "Darlin', remember I'm 77 years old!"

But, the Lord willing (and He has been so good to me), the very next a.m. the Durham Herald-Sun reported that the Duke brain-science department was having a national conference and the main speaker would be Dr. Oliver Sacks, who had written a book called Musicophilia: Tales of Music and the Brain (Knopf, 2007). In his book, Dr. Sacks reported what Dr. Abreu already knew: that music exercises the same parts of the brain as math and science. Of course, I dialed the dean of the brain-science department to ask, though I was not a Duke student, could I puh-leeze attend the conference?

I'll never forget him saying, "Lucia, for $50, we'll let you in." I also heard Dr. Sacks speak again the next night at the Bill Friday Center in Chapel Hill.

I then called the New England Conservatory in Boston and learned it was offering ten fellowships to train people from all over the world in the El Sistema program so they could take it back to their countries. Conservatory Dean Mark Churchill gave me the phone number of a violist with the N.C. Symphony who might be interested, so I invited her to lunch. That's how I met Katie Wyatt. Whoa, talk about chemistry! Katie went to Boston to apply —

along with 200 other people — and she won one of the ten places.

Then Grandma found out the cost of the fellowship was $40,000 — and she had six weeks to raise it! It would take me six months to produce a gala, and that might only raise $20,000. I looked at my sweet husband in his wheelchair, with three daughters of his own, and realized, "no."

While I pondered, the phone rang. It was Dr. Churchill, who told me that the TED Foundation was so impressed with our lovely Katie that it was sending the forty thou!

I asked, "Why would Ted Turner be interested in Durham, N.C.?"

He laughed. "Not Ted Turner, Lucia, but the TED Talks organization." It had been founded in the 1980s to spread good ideas in Technology, Entertainment, and Design (so, T-E-D) and has since grown to include all sorts of cultural projects.

So, Katie went up to Boston, and when she came back we started an El Sistema program in Durham in 2010 under the name "KidzNotes." It has since expanded to Raleigh and Chapel Hill. Now, only seven years later, Katie has been made National Director of El Sistema USA, and its headquarters has been moved from Boston to the South ...

To North Carolina ...

To Durham ...

To Duke University ... not to the Music Department, but to the School of Social Sciences!

Why there? Study after study has shown that this early training keeps at-risk children in school, off the streets, off drugs, out of gangs and out of prison. Keeping just one person in prison costs the taxpayers of North Carolina over $42,000 per year! That's for "three hots and a cot," with no education. In New York, it's $100,000. All money that could go to the public schools instead. Am I preaching? So be it.

Now we're waiting — waiting to see who Katie hires to take her place in the Triangle when she steps over to Duke and waiting to see what El Sistema and KidzNotes can accomplish next.

(And waiting to see if Grandma will ever slowdown.)

P.S.: As this book was being completed, KidzNotes announced that its new Executive Director would be Nick

Malinowski, Program Director of the nonprofit apprenticeship program Citizen Schools and former Community Programs Manager for the Seattle Opera!

For more information on Nick go to

https://www.kidznotes.org/staff-member/nick-malinowski/ ✦

41

Looney Tunes
(2007)

Does any art form we study come back to haunt us in our later years? I submit it does. Those lessons come roaring back to bless or haunt us, and here is why I'm convinced it happens:

My conscientious mother started me off with dance lessons, ballet, and tap at age 5. Through the years I ended up dancing solo in my college May Day program, doing ballet around the May Pole every year in college, and teaching ballet and tap for the Williamston Recreation Department in my forties. When Tony Holland, our mechanic at Crown Volvo Repair Department, learned I loved the old original shag dancing, which originated at Ocean Drive beach where I learned it in high school, he insisted that he and his wife would invite me to the next Seniors Shag Convention. "I'll be the oldest person there!" I whined. He said not. What a way to leave this old world, shagging to Beach Music, removed mentally to a "zone," feeling and smelling the salt air blowing in off the warm, forgiving, summer Atlantic Ocean.

Painting, drawing, coloring: After I won a second-grade prize at Watts Street school here in Durham for drawing and coloring a picture of Jack and the Beanstalk, I was led to believe I could be an artist if I wished. The clincher was that I drew patches on Jack's pants' knees to indicate he was poor. My mother must have figured, "The devil is in the details."

The horror of it is that all my life now, I can't just furnish a room or rooms in the six houses I've lived in during my two marriages; I have to "do" a room. I've designed four residences — three houses, one condo — and "decorated" three beach condos. The colors have to work, the period, the placement of the furnishings. Oh mercy, I forgot: My lawyer daughter let me decorate — with our old stuff — the eleven rooms in our 1912 bed and breakfast, Haughton Hall, down in eastern Carolina near the Roanoke River. It has three bedrooms offered for rent: the Dover Room (very British), the Nags Head Room (old beach-cottage style), and the Jade Room (leans toward Oriental greens and coral red). See? I'm sick. I must be. \

And the music! Early piano and singing lessons evolved into singing leads in high school musicals; singing "Je dis'," Micaela's aria from Carmen, in the Miss America pageant representing Georgia; followed by singing "Night and Day" and "Begin the Beguine" when I was soprano soloist with Phil Spitalny and his All-Girl Orchestra and Chorus on tour from New York to the Paradise Room in Atlanta.

I sang a coloratura soprano solo with the Atlanta Symphony Orchestra under the direction of Robert Shaw — the high point of my life singing "Ah, fors' é lui" from La Traviata in Italian!

Off and on the next 40 years, I directed adult and children's choirs at church. (Gave my paycheck back to the church; ain't I wonderful?) I was a member of the Raleigh Oratorio Society accompanied by the North Carolina Symphony and sang with them at Carnegie Hall accompanied by the New York Symphony. I also played Daisy Mae in the musical Li'l Abner in summer theatre when I was 32.

So, what do I have left from studying the Arts? Besides a Bachelor of Fine Arts Degree in Speech and Drama (oh, I forgot about that), I taught Romper Room on local CBS TV before I married. (Was it acting? Not exactly; I just "played" myself!) Later taught speech, drama, creative writing and filmmaking at the high school level, and art and music from kindergarten through fifth grade.

At 76, what I have left is melodies sticking in my head for hours, sometimes days at a time! Please assure me this happens to everybody. Please. Otherwise, I'm convinced I'm losing it. Going crazy. Through the years the melodies have ranged from, yes, "Through the Years" (often sung at weddings), Chopin's Prelude in E minor, and selections from the Three Bs — Bach, Beethoven, and Brahms — down to Sondheim's "Send In the Clowns" from A Little Night Music and his "Comedy Tonight" from ... the title is too long. (Okay: A Funny Thing Happened on the Way to the Forum.) Last week, for three days my mind listened to, don't laugh, "The sun'll come out tomorrow, betcha' bottom dollah that tomorrah ... there'll be sun. Toooomorrow, tomorrow, there's always tomorrow...!" from Annie.

You don't think I'm a nut, yet?

I call them my "Loony Tunes."

P.S., 2007: Studies show that artists, particularly musicians, live longer than other people. If you don't believe it, go hear Alan Neilson direct the Durham Symphony. He quit telling his age. ✦

42

Third Base
(April 27, 2008)

Hot dang! Upon reaching age 77, I just rounded third base! Don't we live life in quarters? Bases: 25, 50, 75, 100. If living to be 100 is my goal, which it is not, I'm over three-quarters of the way there!

But, if I'm just to be waited upon by my four daughters, or a sweet, patient ol' husband — if I could not read, write, or feed myself — please, Lord, take me Home!

I would not miss TV, bridge — or computers! No problem.

Just take me early (but not immediately).

Yours,

Grandma Lucia ✝

43

Out to Pasture
(2017)

Translated to: "My family (and doctor) is moving Grandma to — are you ready? — Croasdaile Farms! Now if that is not "out to pasture," please tell me what is!

Actually, the real name of my new residence, a retirement community, is just plain, nice Croasdaile Village, but it is in a lovely (I must admit) development named Croasdaile Farms — possibly because, near the impressive entrance, over on the left, is a large field featuring giant old oak trees, two large old barns, two silos and five beautiful black Angus cows. How's that for an artist to paint?

Anyway, back to the subject — what was the subject? Oh, yes, Grandma being sent out to pasture! Well, I guess that's it. 'Nuff said. ✦

ABOUT THE AUTHOR

Lucia Hutchinson Peel Powe

Lucia Hutchinson Peel Powe is the author of two novels, *Roanoke Rock Muddle* (2003) and *The Osprey's View* (2016).

She earned her BFA in speech and drama at Wesleyan Conservatory in Macon, Georgia, and later attended UNC-Chapel, Duke and East Carolina University for graduate work.

Eastern North Carolinians may remember her as "Miss Lucia" on the syndicated program Romper Room produced in Greenville, N.C. Over the years she has taught creative writing, speech, drama, filmmaking, music, art and art history at both the college and high-school levels.

One of her favorite memories was performing as a coloratura soprano with the Atlanta Symphony at the Fox Theatre.

Along with her first husband, Judge Elbert "Junie" Peel of Williamston, Lucia reared four daughters, one horse, six dogs, and three cats.

Widowed for ten years, she married another attorney, E.K. Powe III of Durham, who had three girls. Since her second husband's death in 2011, she has devoted herself to writing and charitable work.

In 2009, she founded KidzNotes, the Triangle branch of "El Sistema," a worldwide nonprofit program that helps at-risk schoolchildren excel by teaching them to play and love classical music.

Grandma Lucia, as she likes to be called, can be reached via email at luciapeelpowe@gmail.com.

ABOUT THE ARTIST

V.C. Rogers

V.C. (for Virginius Cullum) Rogers is a semi-retired freelance cartoonist in Durham, N.C. A native of Bennettsville, South Carolina, Rogers earned degrees in English at Davidson College and UNC-Chapel Hill.

He spent most of the 1980s at the Durham Morning Herald and from 1997 to 2018 was a political cartoonist for the Triangle's Indy Weekly. His work has won top honors in the Association of Alternative Newsmedia Awards four times, most recently in 2018.

He has been a member of the Association of American Editorial Cartoonists since 1980 and served twelve years as its Secretary-Treasurer. His history of the AAEC's first fifty years was published for Association's Golden Anniversary celebration in 2007.

He is currently writing a history of newspaper and magazine parodies.

Lucia Peel Powe's other books

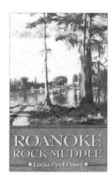

Lucia Peel Powe

The Osprey's View

"What does an osprey diving for fish and causing an awful boating accident on the Roanoke River have to do with a romance years later in Richmond and Milan?

Follow the sly stylings of Lucia Peel Powe in her novella *The Osprey's View*, watch closely as she reveals many keen observations of life and love, of surprises and reversals, in the World War II-era South, and be nicely rewarded indeed." — Bland Simpson, author of *Little Rivers* & *Waterway Tales*.

Roanoke Rock Muddle

"This book will make you long for a view of the Albemarle Sound and a taste of oyster pie." — Lee Smith, author of *The Last Girls*.

Both books are available on Amazon.com and in fine bookstores everywhere.